CADD

SUPER HATCHES

Hatch Guide
for the
United States

Carl Richards and
Bob Braendle

Illustrations by Eric Jon Peterson

CADDIS SUPER HATCHES

Hatch Guide
for the
United States

Carl Richards and
Bob Braendle
Illustrations by Eric Jon Peterson

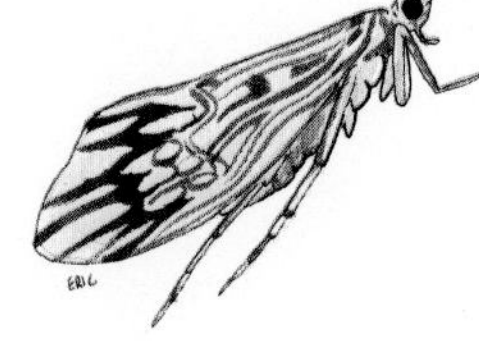

Published in 1997 by
Frank Amato Publications, Inc.
PO Box 82112
Portland, Oregon 97282
(503) 653-8108

Softbound
ISBN: 1-57188-078-X
UPC: 0-66066-00275-4
Hardbound
ISBN: 1-57188-079-8
UPC: 0-66066-00276-1

Front cover inset photograph: Jim Schollmeyer

Illustrations: Eric Jon Peterson

Book design: Tony Amato

Printed in Hong Kong

1 3 5 7 9 10 8 6 4 2

Contents

Acknowledgments

We would like to thank Dr. Brian Armitage of the Ohio Biological Station, Columbus, Ohio for identifying our caddisfly collection species. We are grateful to Dr. Jeff Cooper of the Water Resources Institute, Grand Valley State University and Larry Solomon of New York for sending scientific papers.

Every book of this type builds on the work of others, we would like to thank Larry Solomon and Eric Leiser for the first book on caddis, *Caddis and the Angler*, which solved many of the mysteries of these insects, Gary LaFontaine for his monumental work, *Caddisflies*, to John Juracek and Craig Mathews for their excellent little book, *Fishing the Yellowstone Hatches,* and to John Shewey for his fine work, *Mastering The Spring Creeks*.

We would also like to express our appreciation to our wives Alecia Richards and Anna Maria Clark for their patience and understanding. To Fred Vargas for help in testing the patterns and Glen Blackwood for suggestions on the text. Special thanks to Bill Heckle, the very talented fly tier from Aurora, Illinois, for introducing us to the Tape Wing Caddis which has become one of our favorite adult caddis patterns.

Introduction

It was mid-May on the Au Sable River and we were searching for *Chimarra atterrima* (Tiny Black Caddis), which are supposed to be important in the spring. There were small black caddisflies crawling out of the river onto the dock and banks of Club Ginger Quill as can be expected with *C. atterrima*. The fish however were feeding midstream on emergers and adults. We wondered if they were *Chimarra* females laying eggs. Further examination determined, (there were pupal shucks present in the water), that they were hatching adults and the fish were selectively feeding on pupae and emerging adults in midstream.

Later that evening we keyed the caddis we had caught. There were no *Chimarra,* but many *Brachycentrus lateralis* (Little Black Caddis) and *Dolophilodes distinctus* (Tiny Black Gold Speckled Caddis). The Little Black Caddis were emerging midstream and the Gold Speckled Caddis were crawling out on the dock. We never did find any *Chimarra* and do not believe they are important, at least not here. Both of the caddisflies we did find looked similar when they were flying but their habits of emergence were very different. Obviously this was not what we expected to find. At this point we realized how important it was to be able to identify caddisflies to the genus, if not the species, level. Both of these caddisflies appear very similar on the wing but the actions of each are very different. Knowing the habits of these two caddisflies would have aided us greatly. *D. distinctus* swim to land as a pupa, where they shed their shuck. *B. lateralis,* on the other hand, swim to the surface as a pupa and hatch midstream at the water's surface, they drift anywhere from five to over 20 feet before flying away. The two species must be fished in different ways.

The next day the hatch began as expected. Carl had several fish take the pupa fished on a dropper below an adult. I found a couple of fish feeding on hatching adults in a slower side channel. Most of these fish refused the traditional patterns I presented to them, but all ate the tape and feather winged adult pattern, including a 12-inch brook trout which took the fly a number of times after I had hooked it for a few seconds (I was eight feet away and had a clear view of the whole pool). I was dumbfounded when the same fish took the fly again and again. That imitation must have looked and acted very much like the real insect. This pattern has become one of our favorites.

These and other experiences during caddis hatches caused us to research existing material, both angling and scientific. Two things became very apparent; 1) Traditional patterns and techniques are not consistently effective during a caddis hatch and; 2) Knowing the caddisflies, at least to the genus level, and their habits of emergence and egg-laying is imperative in order to effectively fish these hatches.

We needed a quick, easy way to identify the insects at streamside. The problem with scientific keys is the need for extensive lab equipment, the difficulties in their use and the time it takes to use them.

We found we could not rely on scientific papers for descriptions because the workers were almost never keying out freshly hatched caddisflies. They examine specimens in alcohol, sometimes months later when color can be drastically changed. Some such as Dr. Oliver S. Flint, Jr. of the Smithsonian keep good field notes and note when they are examining specimens in alcohol, but many do not. This scientific data has been the primary source for almost every angling work on the subject, and a lot of the color descriptions are dead wrong because of relying on these writings.

Another problem the angler faces is knowing how the natural is going to act and at what stage it is most vulnerable to the fish. The scientific works do not help us there, this knowledge can only come from identifying the insect and from keen observation of the actions of the caddisflies and the fish.

Some fishing books state that caddisflies are of lesser importance than mayflies, with the possible exception of tailwater fisheries, but many studies have found caddisflies to be a primary food source on a variety of rivers. There are correlations to be made based on water type, water temperature, amount of food present and flow rates, but no one can deny that at times caddisflies are the most important insect to trout. Some rivers are mainly caddis rivers and many of these are the best trout streams in the country. Try fishing the Bighorn in the fall and you will know what we mean. Knowing the caddis hatch you are fishing to will not only help you match their appearance, but knowing the expected behavior will allow you to fish your imitation in a manner consistent with the natural's behavior.

The one almost insurmountable problem in understanding which caddis species you are fishing to is the listing of hundreds and hundreds of species. No one could possibly keep in their memory the habits and appearances of all the species written about. It is possible, however, to be completely familiar with the few caddisflies which are important in your area. In fact, it is vital for consistent success. Since the total number of caddisfly species is mind boggling we set out to discover which ones are really important to the angler, that is, which species cause heavy feeding by trout for at least a one week period in cool, running water. We call these species the super caddisflies, or the caddis super hatches. As it turned out surprisingly few species fulfilled our criteria for each region, (ten or twelve). Some genera such as *Hydropsyche* have as many as 70 species which are true super caddis but look alike and act very much alike when emerging and ovipositing, so the particular species does not really matter, it is enough to know just the genus. Some genera have one, two or three important species which act alike but do not look alike. It is important to know these to the species level. All in all we believe we have reduced the number of important caddisflies to a manageable few for each region of the country. These are listed and an easy method of identification is provided. We have also included many species which cannot be called super caddis, at least by us, but do occasionally produce good rises and may even be super caddis on some rivers. If your river does have caddisflies, means of easy identification of these insects and their habits and appearance can be found in the last half of this book.

Chapter 1

THE BIOLOGY OF CADDISFLIES

Understanding the Vulnerable Stages

The life cycle of the caddisfly is known as a "complete metamorphosis". In a complete metamorphosis there are four stages: egg, larva, pupa and adult. This life cycle differs from mayflies which undergo an incomplete metamorphosis that consists of egg, nymph and adult. Caddis hatches are notoriously more difficult for the angler to master than mayfly hatches. The fact that caddisflies have a pupal stage complicates fishing to a caddis emergence for reasons which will be explained later. The fact that caddisflies do not have a final molt or spinner stage like mayflies further complicates fishing these insects since the angler cannot tell an emerging adult from an adult female flying off after returning to the surface when egg laying. They look alike but the silhouette of the ascending pupa and that of the adult are very different.

CYCLE OF A HATCH

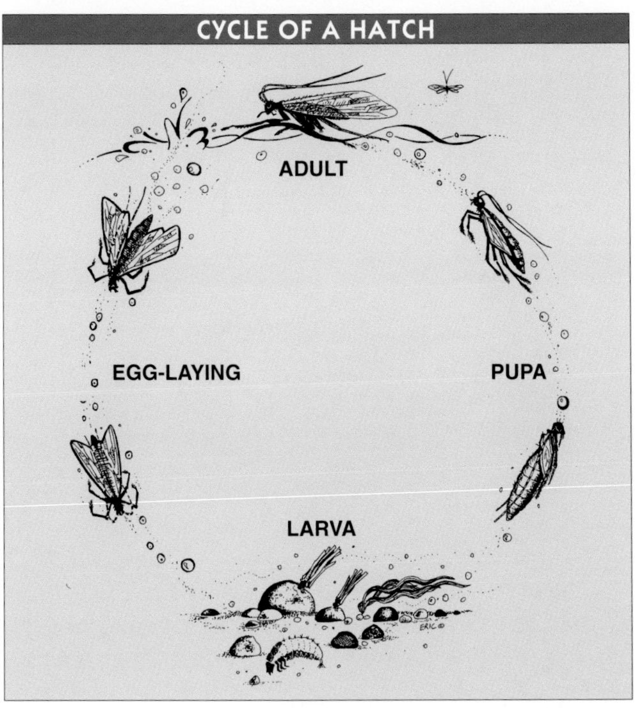

Caddisfly eggs are fertilized on shore and deposited in the river or on shore near the river. These eggs hatch into larvae which become the first stage of interest to the angler. The larvae of most species build cases of some sort. These cases aid in the identification of caddisflies because of their design and construction which is consistent within the family and genera. Some families build a net used to filter food from the water and a silken retreat near the net. Including Hydropsychidae, the most important family of caddisflies to the angler, these are called net builders. Family Rhyacophilidae on the other hand is a free-living larva. These crawl around naked on the bottom without a case until just before pupation. At that time all caddisflies construct a case in which the larva turns into a pupa.

LARVA AND SEVERAL CASES

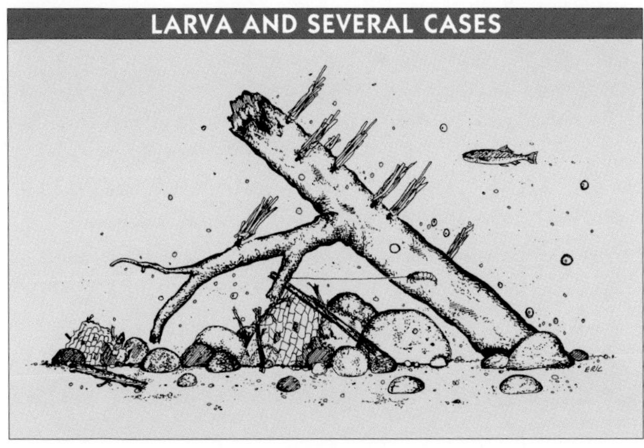

The larva is the longest period in the life of a caddisfly and usually lasts about 30 weeks. Most species spend a good portion of this time in a case. These cased larva are available to trout year-round. Some studies have found a surprisingly large percentage of the trout's diet consists of cased caddis larva. Larva mature in stages called instars. For those caddis larvae that build cases,

one of two things must happen as they grow; either an addition to the case must be built or a new case constructed. When the latter occurs, the naked larva may drift to a new location which makes the naked worm available to the trout. Add to this the phenomena of behavioral drift (a period of larval drift which occurs before dawn and after dusk) and we see larva are a plentiful and reliable food source and stomach analysis shows trout do eat a lot of them.

LARVAL DRIFT

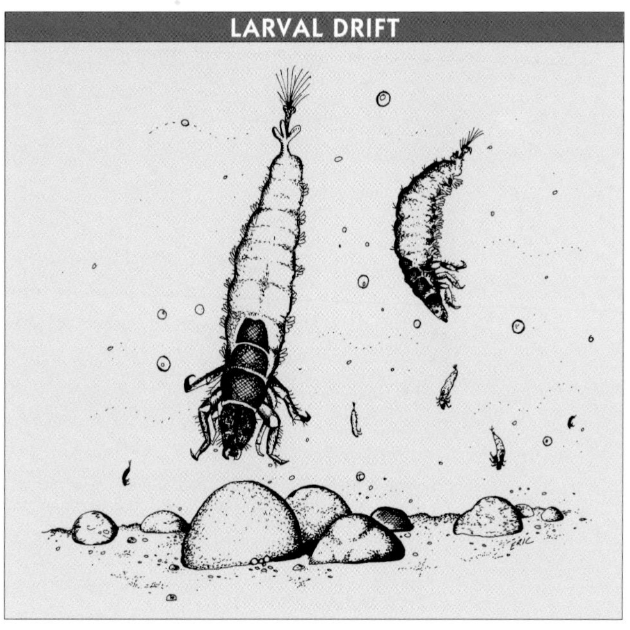

Larvae are small grub-like worms with a dark head. Short legs are attached to the thoracic segment behind the head and an anal process is usually present, located at the end of the abdomen. This anal process is used to swim with as the insect wiggles its body. Larvae swim upside down, the anal process is up and the head is down. Body colors fall into five general shades, green, tan, gray, cream and yellow. The first three are colors of the roamers and netspinners, the latter two are case builders. Head colors are variegated light and dark brown and the dorsal of the thoracic segments are tan to dark brown. Length ranges from 2mm to 35mm depending on the species and degree of maturity. The mature larva is longer than the adult it will become.

FISH FEEDING ON PUPAE

Once the larva has matured, it seals its case so that only enough water to provide the necessary oxygen can penetrate, and then begins its pupal stage. At this point free-living and net-building caddisflies also build cases. This sealed case, attached to the substrate, is a sure sign that an emergence is close, usually within a few weeks. Through case identification and dissecting the case to discover the degree of pupal maturity, you can tell what fly will be hatching and the approximate date of the emergence. When the eyes of the pupa turn black the insect is close to emerging.

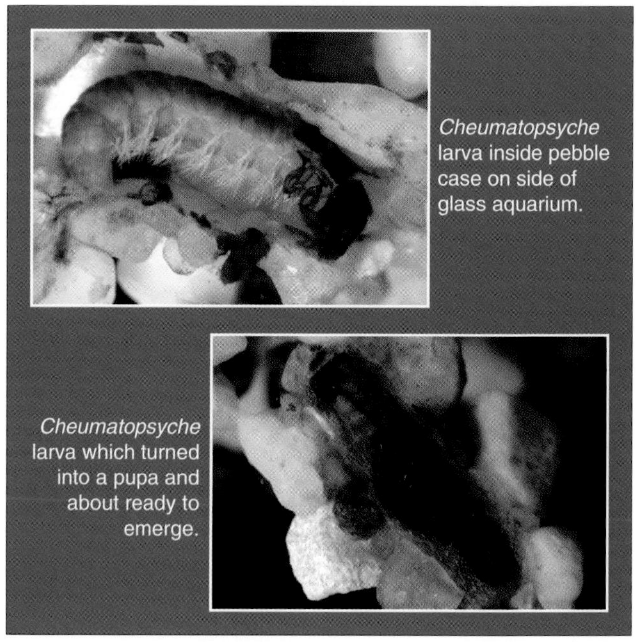

Cheumatopsyche larva inside pebble case on side of glass aquarium.

Cheumatopsyche larva which turned into a pupa and about ready to emerge.

A mature pupa will have the body color of the adult it will hatch into although the body color will be a little lighter and brighter and the wing cases will be darker due to the wings being compacted in the pupal case. A mature pupa is a fully developed adult contained in a thin almost transparent sheath called a pupal shuck. Length ranges from 1mm to 30mm depending on the species.

PUPA

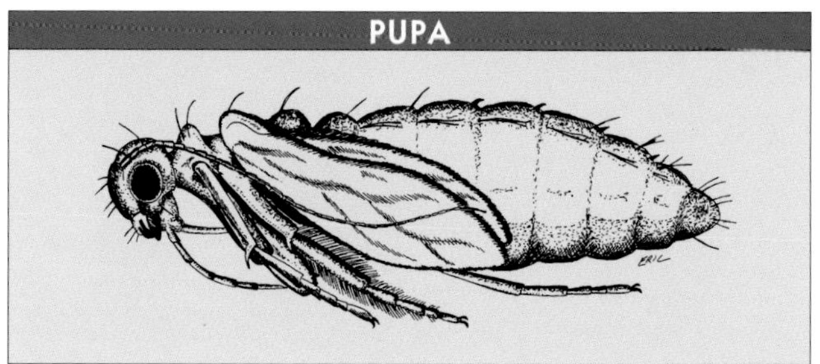

When mature the pupa chews its way free of the case. It often drifts close to the bottom for a period of time before beginning its ascent to the surface by swimming with its middle legs. These legs are adapted for swimming

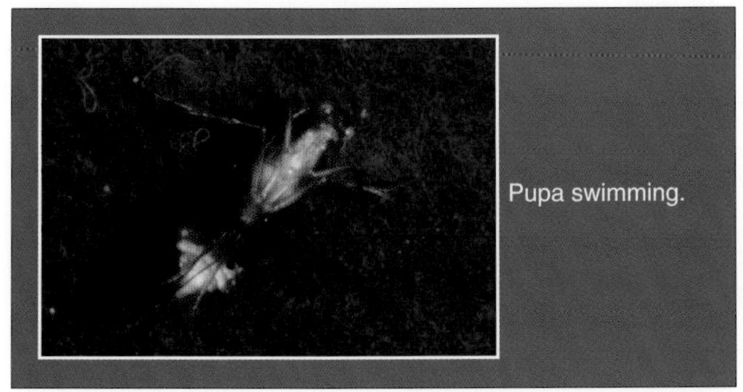
Pupa swimming.

by possessing fringes of hair at the ends. This is the beginning of an extremely vulnerable period of the pupal stage. A successfully emerging pupa will usually penetrate the surface film on its first attempt and begin struggling out from the shuck. This struggle can take from five seconds to a minute or longer. This time period will allow the insect to drift from 10 to 30 feet or more downstream. This is the most vulnerable stage of all. After freeing itself completely from the shuck, the winged insect will fly from the surface very quickly. Two or three flaps of the wings and it is off the water.

SWIMMING PUPA

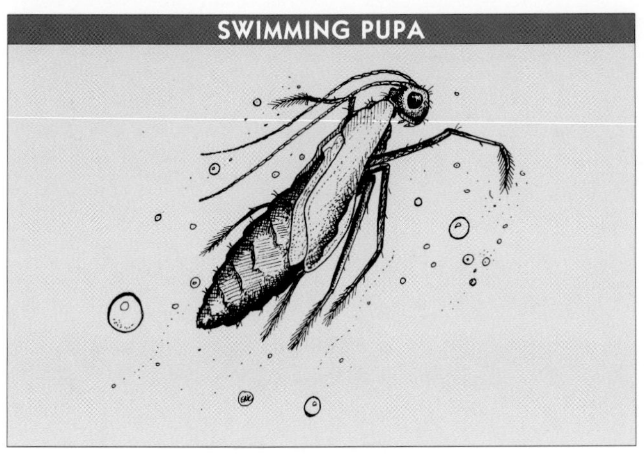

Pupae which are unsuccessful on the first attempt, (this can be a large percentage), drift just under the surface or sink back down to the bottom, regain their strength and try to penetrate the surface film again. The failure rate increases proportionally with each unsuccessful attempt. In this fatigued condition many will not have the strength to penetrate the surface and/or escape the pupal shuck. The ones that become stuck in the shuck are called crippled or stillborn caddisflies.

EMERGING PUPA

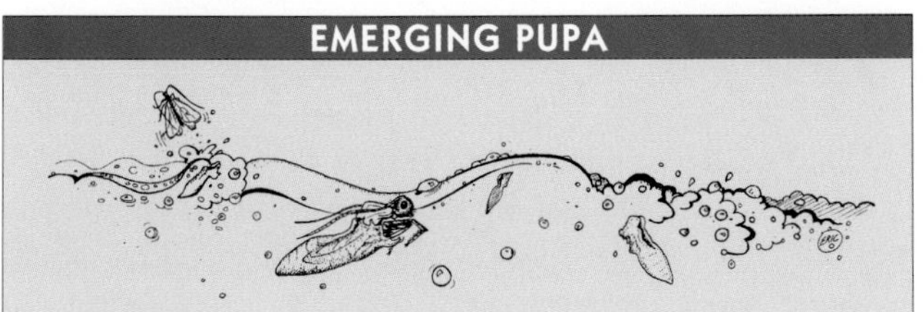

Some species do not emerge in the typical manner. The family Philopotomidae, for instance, has a genus which crawls out of the river to hatch (*Chimarra*), and one that swims to the surface as a pupa and then walks on the water as a pupa to shore (*Dolophilodes*). The latter has wingless females in winter and spring but they are winged in summer. Neither genus seems to hatch in great numbers at any one time, but *Dolophilodes* are present all year and trout feed on them when nothing else is available.

SWIMMING PUPA AND WINGLESS FEMALE

The factors that contribute to the success rate of pupae emerging are, at best, only somewhat identifiable. For instance it is much easier for a pupa to penetrate the surface film in broken water. Slow water with scum on the surface inhibits penetration of the surface. In addition water type, temperature (insects do not fly well in cold weather) and oxygen levels, all have an effect on the length of time it takes a caddis to emerge from a pupa to an adult.

Swarm of caddisflies, (*B. lateralis*), on the Au Sable River in Michigan. The white splotches in the picture are caddisflies.

If a caddis achieves emergence it then lives on the banks of the river from two to eight weeks, sustaining itself on moisture collected from leaves, nectar, as well as drinking from the river itself.

Adult caddisflies typically have a body length approximately 70 percent of their overall length (head to wing tip).

Caddis have four wings longer than the body which in flight make them appear much larger than they really are. Anglers constantly overestimate the size of the artificial needed when fishing to a hatch of caddisflies. The true size is best judged by catching one. Body color varies somewhat even in the same species and is also best decided by close inspection. Males and females may have different body colors due to the underlying egg mass of the females. Two antennae are present and their length can be valuable in identification. Caddisflies fly erratically and appear as if they can't fly straight. They also fly quickly which makes it difficult to catch them without a net, (the bigger the net the better).

After mating along the river bank, females renew the life cycle by depositing fertilized eggs back into the water in one of four methods: 1) bouncing on the water and dipping their abdomen into the river, releasing the eggs, 2) diving, 3) crawling under the surface to lay the eggs on the substrate, or 4) laying eggs on objects close to water so rain washes them into the water.

FEMALE DIPPING EGGS ON SURFACE AND SWIMMING UP AFTER CRAWLING UNDER WATER

Females may mate two or more times before dying. Those that crawl under water to oviposit may return two or more times to the surface. This further complicates matters for the angler as the profile of the female swimming up to surface and the pupa swimming up to the surface to emerge are very different. The angler can't tell the difference between them because the adults flying off the surface look alike, but the fish are often keyed to one or the other. After ovipositing is complete, many caddisflies are unable to fly away so they drift spent in the film. Trout relish this because they are easy prey, even though they are not as nutritious after the egg mass has been expelled.

SPENT CADDIS ON THE WATER

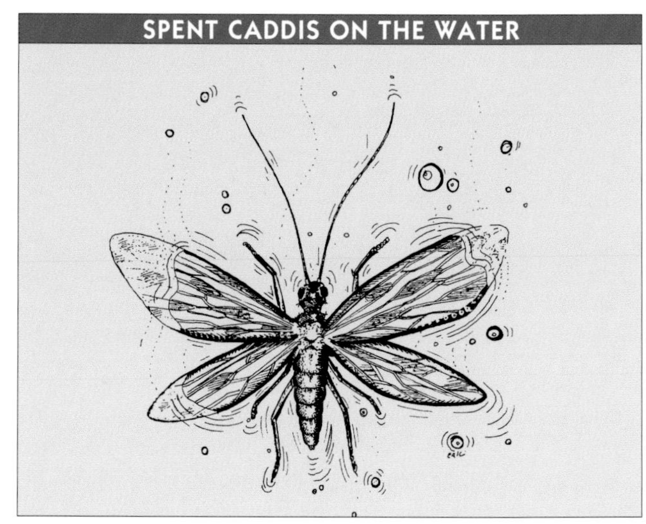

Knowing the egg-laying habits of each family is critical to consistent angling success. The following list will help you identify what is going on and let you choose the proper angling method when casting to trout feeding on ovipositing caddisflies. Of course to use it you must be able to identify a natural to the family level. We will explain how to do this easily later in the book.

Caddisfly Families that Oviposit at the Water's Surface

Glossosomatidae, Helicopsychidae, Lepidostomatidae, Leptoceridae, Molannidae, Odontoceridae, and Phryganidae

Caddisfly Families that Oviposit Underwater

Hydroptilidae, Philopotamidae, Polycentropodidae, Rhyacophilidae, and Psychomyiidae

Caddisflies that Oviposit By Both Methods

Hydropsychidae, Brachycentridae

Limnephilidae is an extremely diverse family. Approximately one half of the species oviposit above the water on rocks and vegetation where rain washes the eggs into the river. The other half dive or crawl under water to oviposit.

Caddisflies can and do cause great rises by trout and some of our best trout rivers are primarily caddis rivers. It is important, at least for us, to know as much as we can about them. They are more difficult to master than mayflies, but we have tried to reduce the number of species to be considered, made it easy to identify those species and simplified as much as possible the fishing tactics needed to consistently hook during caddisfly activity.

Chapter II

CADDIS FISHING STRATEGY

To be successful when fishing a river in which fish are feeding on caddisflies you must first discover what stage of the hatch the fish are feeding on. This is much more difficult to figure out when trout are feeding on caddisflies than when they are feeding on mayflies. This is because caddisflies change very little during their adult lifetime, whereas mayflies change from a dun to a spinner which is a very obvious and visible change. Many species of caddisflies lay their eggs underwater and return to the surface to fly away. Since emerging caddis flying off the water and adult females returning to the surface and flying away look alike, it is necessary to be able to tell the difference as your fishing tactics will differ. Add to this the problem of caddis just flying around, neither hatching nor egg laying and you have a "compound hatch" with only a single insect involved. With so many facets of caddis activity, only through careful observation will you be able to recognize what is occurring.

A 23-inch Muskegon River brown trout caught on a Partridge-Tape Wing Adult.

Trout flashing while deep feeding on the bottom.

When you see few or no fish feeding on the surface pay very close attention to what is happening under the surface. Look for the "flashes" of a fish turning on its side and note at what depth this activity is taking place. If it is happening in the lower 1-24 inches and is regular, fish are probably feeding on the pre-emergence drift of the pupa or on larva. If the activity is in the upper 1-12 inches, it is likely that fish are feeding on the pupae as they swim to the surface and are drifting sub-surface. In this situation there will probably be some insects flying as well but they can be difficult to see, especially small, dark forms. Very little feeding takes place midstream, most feeding is either bottom or top.

BROOK TROUT BOTTOM FEEDING ON PUPAE

When you see fish feeding on the surface, the choice is between hatching caddis and adult females returning to the surface after laying eggs. It is impossible to tell the difference between the two adult stages by looking at the insect from a distance. In the case of females that oviposit by diving or crawling under the water's surface, swim back up to the surface and then fly away (more behave in this manner than not), casual observance of the insect's behavior is not going to be the key to discovering what is going on. The only sure answer to this question is the presence of pupal shucks on the surface, which during any super hatch of streamborne caddis will be easily visible to the naked eye. Conversely, if there are no shucks but the fish are feeding consistently, it is most likely an egg-laying flight. There can be and often is an emergence and ovipositing going on at the same time. Trout sometimes prefer egg-laying females to the emerging pupae but the silhouette of the two stages are very different.

RAINBOWS FEEDING ON TOP

The other situation which will cause consistent feeding, generally without the presence of flying caddisflies, is when spent caddis drift on the water after dying, this should be relatively easy to recognize by observing them on the water. These situations can happen in any combination, but with careful observation you should be able to isolate the particular situations you are dealing with. Once you know what is occurring, you can apply the following strategies to improve your success during a caddis super hatch.

LARVA NET WITH RETREAT

Fishing the Larvae

When larvae (worms) drift, they do so with their heads and legs down and tails up. They wiggle their bodies to raise themselves in the water, therefore we need a pattern which will allow for this type of presentation (Wiggle Worm). There are many techniques to fish this stage effectively. Our favorites include: the use of a strike indicator and weight or a weighted fly. With this technique you control the depth of the fly by moving the strike indicator up or down the leader accordingly, or by varying the amount of weight. You may also use the Leisenring lift. A cast is made

STRIKE INDICATOR

upstream and across the current and, as the fly drifts downstream, the rod is lifted to keep excess line off the water, minimizing the chance of drag. Lower the rod as the fly drifts past to feed more line to the drift. Other strategies include an upstream cast and stripping the line in as the fly drifts back to you. A strike indicator can be valuable with this method as well. Any of the techniques you use when nymph fishing with mayflies will perform well during a behavioral drift, with the possible exception of swimming the nymph to the surface at the end of the drift.

LARVA ON STRIKE INDICATOR RIG

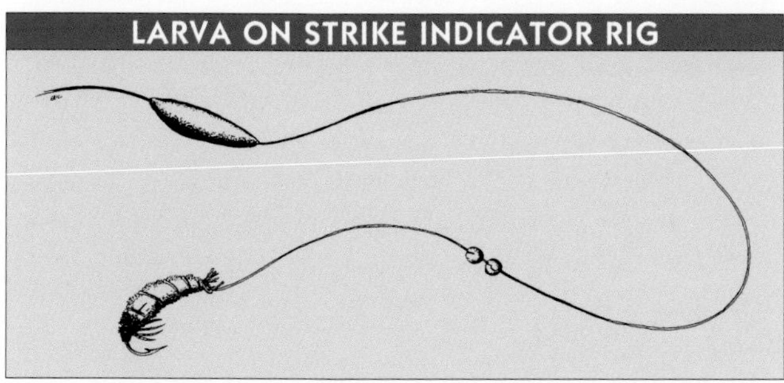

MENDING

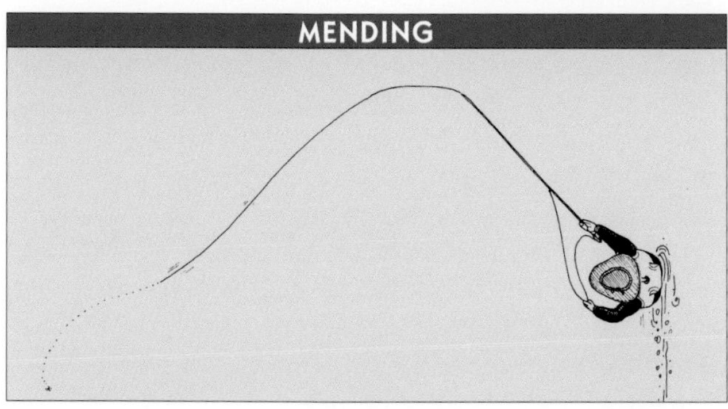

Any of these basic techniques may be improved by mending the line which will reduce the likelihood of drag and extend the effective drift. In addition to mending, the use of the reach, curve, slack line and other advanced casting techniques can be invaluable to these and any other stream strategies. If you find these techniques are difficult or unknown to you, see your local fly shop for advice or instruction.

CURVE CAST

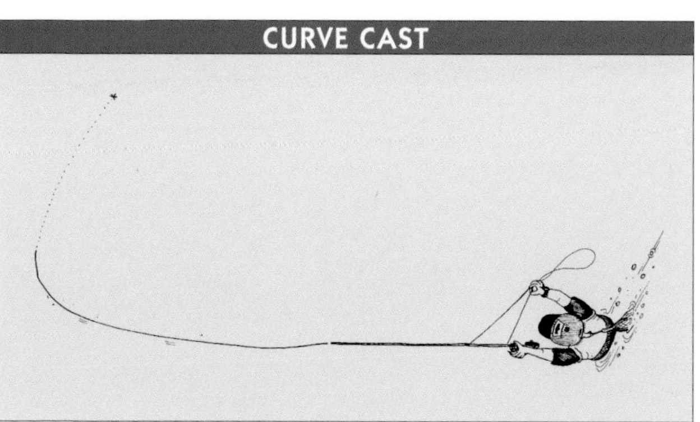

Fishing the Emergence

If there is a hatch, (there are shucks in the surface film), there are several different stages available to the fish at this time: pupae, emergers, adults and stillborn or crippled caddis.

Carl Richards with 22-inch rainbow caught on a Bob's Teardrop Emerger.

When mature, pupae chew themselves free of their cases. They drift from zero to hundreds of feet on the bottom before swimming to the surface and becoming suspended in the film where they drift for 5-20 feet or more as they split the back of their pupal shuck to emerge and fly quickly away.

Some species crawl along the bottom and out of the river to hatch on dry land (*Chimarra*), while others swim to the surface and walk on top of the water to land as pupae and begin to emerge *(Dolophilodes distinctus)*. These insects must be fished in a manner that is suitable for imitating their actions. This is why knowing the caddis, at least to the family level, and preferably to the genus level, is imperative to successfully fishing the hatch.

Fishing the pupa during its pre-emergence drift is identical to fishing the larva with the addition of swimming to the surface at the end of the drift. Keep in mind that a drifting pupa will have its legs at rest under its body. A swimming pupa will have its middle legs rowing back and forth like a skuller.

Bob Braendle fishing the best trout stream in the Appalachian mid-south.

The most vulnerable point in the hatch is when the pupae are drifting, suspended in the film, trying to escape their pupal skin. Fish feeding on this stage appear to be feeding on dry flies or adults. Stomach content analysis shows pupae far outnumber adults in fish caught during the hatch. This means they have been feeding on the pre-emergence drift on the bottom and the subsurface drift during the emergence, long before they feed on emergers.

To fish the subsurface pupal drift most effectively the classic drag-free float is employed. Combining casting strategy with mending to provide accurate, realistic presentation with the correct imitation, you will undoubtedly enjoy success. The only problem with fishing a suspended pupa is that of visibility, to eliminate this problem use an adult caddis and tie the pupa on as a dropper. This allows you to pinpoint the location of your fly as well as helping to confirm which stage of the hatch each fish is keyed in to. It often varies from fish to fish.

SLACK LINE CAST

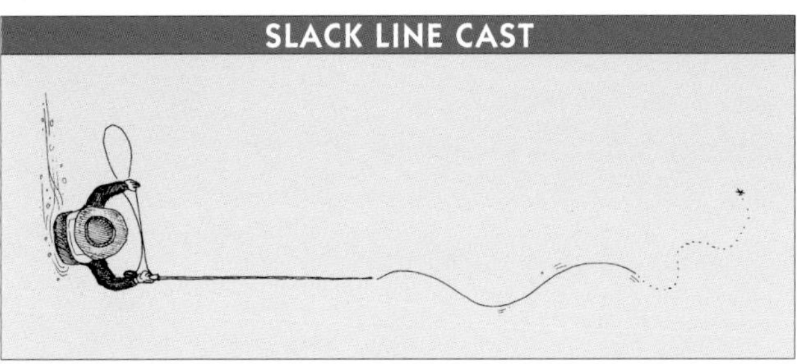

DROPPER RIG

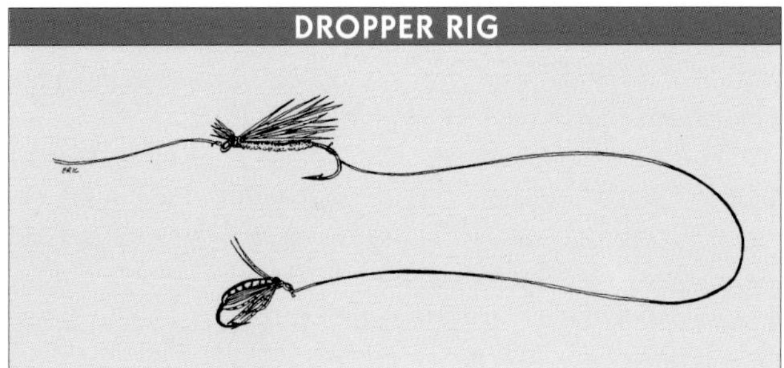

The emerger and/or stillborn caddis (which is the same imitation) are also fished with a drag-free float but with the addition of a minute wiggle or shake which simulates the struggle of the insect trying to free itself from the shuck. This struggle is visible to the angler and the fish. It can trigger the instincts of trout to strike your imitation. This wiggle must be just subtle enough to move the fly but not to disrupt the downstream drift. This palsied dead drift has accounted for the largest fish of many trips to the river as well as saving a few otherwise fishless days.

The adult caddisfly is on the water for an extremely short period of time. Once out of the shuck, it's two or three flaps of the wings and the insect is off the water. The use of an adult imitation at this point in the hatch is probably going to be less effective than a pupa or emerger, but they can still provide some excellent fishing.

Fishing to Egg-Laying Caddisflies

Rising fish may be feeding on adult females that have come back to the river to lay their eggs. This can happen in any one of four methods: 1) females bounce on the water's surface, dipping their abdomens into the water to release fertile eggs, 2) females crawl under the water using sticks, logs, rocks, or your legs to lay eggs under water. (The gelatinous green slime you find on your waders after fishing is probably caddis eggs), 3) females can dive and swim underwater to lay eggs on the bottom. These females may return to the surface, fly away and return back to the river many times. In the fourth method, females lay their eggs on objects close to the water where they will be washed into the water by rain. This method does not allow the fish any chance to feed on the insects.

The first of these methods can be successfully imitated by "shotgunning" your imitation directly on top of a feeding fish. This hit-'em-on-the-head technique can provide some quick, exciting strikes. Skittering an adult past a riser is also very effective. The rate of speed of the skittering is most important. It cannot be too fast or the fish will not take the fly. Actually the slower the better. The cast is made across stream and the rod tip is twitched. At some point the current will put a belly in the line and the fly will begin to drag. This will speed up the fly so it is dragging too fast. To slow down the speed of the drag, feed line out while still twitching the rod tip. This will greatly increase the length of the effective drift. The most effective method of fishing a pupa is to add a pupal imitation as a dropper to the adult which is to be skittered. This is evidently the perfect action to impart to a pupal imitation. Quite often you have egg-laying females returning to the surface and an emergence occurring at the same time so you may hook fish on both imitations. If trout are feeding on only one form, this technique will allow you to discover which one is being taken.

The other two methods of ovipositing can be effectively simulated by fishing an adult imitation as a wet fly. The fly is allowed to swim using weight on the leader in a traditional "down-and-across wet fly swing". The most productive method for a diving caddis is using weight and an upstream-and-across cast, allowing the fly to sink to the bottom, drift along the bottom and swimming the fly back to the surface. Often the fish hit the fly at the end of the swing or after the swing is over and is hanging in the flow. When females which have been egg-laying on the bottom swim up and break through the surface film, they bounce on the surface a number of times before flying away. The skittering method described above is also deadly.

The last stage of the caddis' life occurs after egg-laying is complete. The females die and once their muscles relax, the wings flatten out and provide a very broad, moth-like silhouette. This typically occurs after dark but can happen in the afternoon early in the season. There are often many spent flies floating in the early morning, left over from the previous evening, this can provide good dry fly fishing when nothing else is going on. These are fished dead drift.

Author with a 19-inch Bighorn brown caught on a Peeping Caddis.

Chapter III

DESIGNING AND TYING CADDIS PATTERNS

Notes On Tying Caddis Larvae

The larvae of *Hydropsyche, Cheumatopsyche* and *Rhyacophila* are very useful to imitate. The latter is free-living and the first two are common netspinners so all three genera are fairly easy prey for trout because they do not live in cases. Stomach analysis proves fish do eat a lot of them. For some reason very simple imitations are often effective. One example is a brass bead head and a simple spun fur body. The *Hydropsyche* should be tan or gray and the *Cheumatopsyche* and *Rhyacophila* should be green. If exact imitations of larvae are desired they can be constructed by tying-in a spun body and making the head and thorax from liquid latex mixed with acrylic paint in the various colors. Feather fibers can be attached for the legs by dipping the tips of the fibers in a little liquid latex and placing them in position. The latex on the feather will bond to the latex on the thorax almost instantly.

If the pattern is to be fished during the "drift", the fly should be tied "Wiggle" style so it can be swum up and down in the current.

Choosing the Color for Caddis Wings

The wings on naturals are translucent and they appear much lighter when the insect is flying than when the natural is held in the hand. This is because when the wings are folded and held next to the darker body which is opaque, the body will show through somewhat so the wings appear darker. When the trout is looking up at a floating natural the wings are backlighted from the sky, at least some of the light filters through the translucent wings so it also appears lighter to the fish than it does to the angler when the insect is held in the hand. It is very important for the fly tier to take this phenomenon into account when designing a pattern for a particular species.

A very effective winging method is the use of small feathers from various game birds such as quail, partridge, ruffed grouse, ducks, hen hackle, etc. Feathers from these game birds are found on the backs, sides and rumps. These are put on a piece of frosted Scotch tape which is then folded on the stem in the middle of the feather and shaped with scissors. The sticky part of the tape should be painted with Seal-All cement as the cement on the Scotch tape is not waterproof. This winging method produces an extremely realistic caddisfly wing that has a sheen which feathers and hair do not have but the tape does have. It also produces a wing which is semi-translucent like the natural's.

Patterned wings can be made by choosing a feather with the lightest color of the natural's wing and drawing in the darker colors with marking pens or acrylic paint and liquid latex mixed together.

Choosing the Color of Freshly-Hatched Adults

Freshly-hatched caddisflies are lighter in color at the moment of emergence. This is true of both the wings and body. As their exoskeleton hardens, the color rapidly darkens. It is difficult to capture the exact shade of fresh emergents on film because they darken so quickly. This means when you are fishing an emergence you should use a lighter imitation and when fishing to egg-layers a darker one.

Choosing the Color of Caddis Pupae

Since the pupal shuck is translucent, the color of the pupa is the same as the freshly-emerged adult except the wing cases are darker than the wings on the adult because they are compacted in the case.

SPENT DRY AND OVIPOSITING WET PATTERNS

Diving caddis pattern with air-holding CDC wing which imitates the air bubbles an egg-laying female carries while crawling under water.

Antron Spent Caddis with wings of Antron and hackle.

Quad Wing Little Olive Sedge.

Delta Wing Caddis Cinnamon Sedge.

ADULT DRY PATTERNS

Hair Wing Green Sedge with Z-lon underwing to give the pattern some sheen.

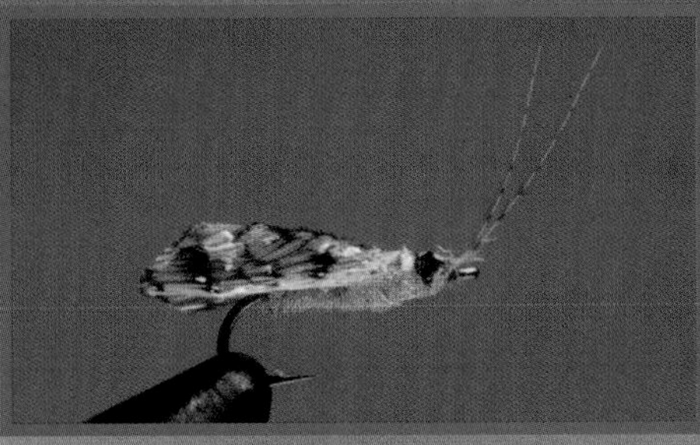
Feather and Tape Wing Little Sister Sedge. Mottling painted on with acrylic paint.

Western Autumn Mottled Sedge with feather tape wing. Mottling painted on with marking pen. (*L. thorus*, Bighorn River).

Feather and Tape Wing Dot Wing Long-horned Sedge, dots are acrylic paint.

Feather and Tape Wing Cinnamon Sedge, dots painted on with acrylic paint.

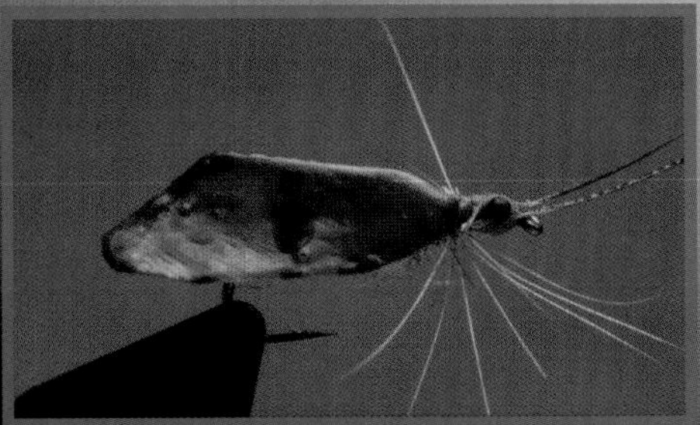
Feather and Tape Wing Great Autumn Sedge, pattern from acrylic paint.

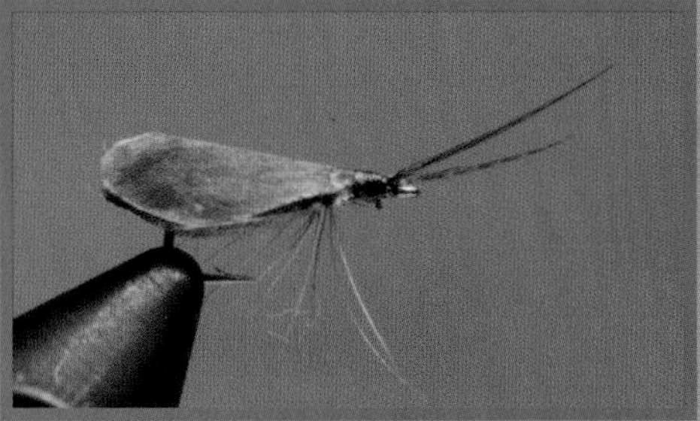

Feather and Tape Wing Tiny Black Caddis.

Feather and Tape Wing Little Black Caddis.

Two Feather Wing Black Long Horned Sedge with two strands of Krystal Flash for sheen.

Air Through Wing Little Black Caddis.

Feather and Tape Wing Dot Wing Sedge.

Fly Film Wing Cinnamon Sedge.

EMERGERS

Quick and Dirty Cinnamon Sedge Emerger.

Snow Show Rabbit Wing Cinnamon Sedge Emerger.

Down Wing Emerger Zebra Caddis.

CDC WIng Little Olive Sedge Emerger.

Folded Deer Hair Little Olive Emerger.

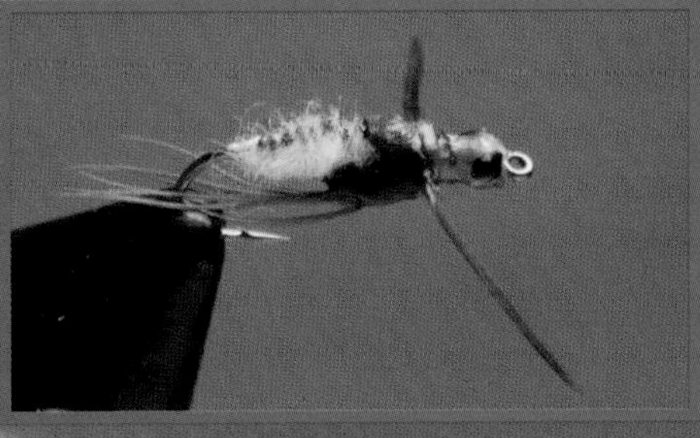

Latex Wing Case Little Olive Sedge Pupa (with darker dorsal).

PUPAE

Z-lon Wing Case Cinnamon Sedge Pupa.

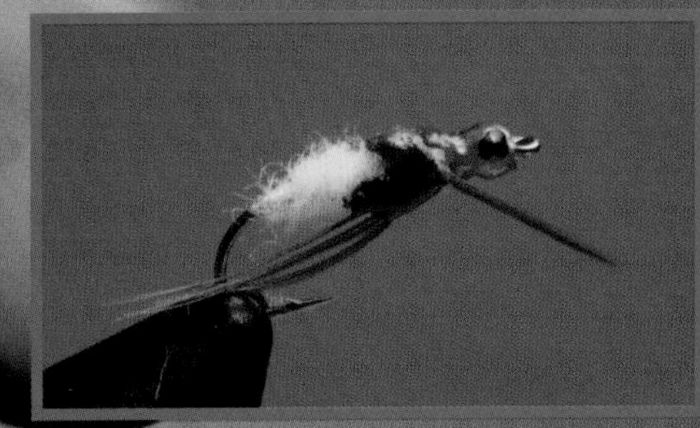

Latex Wing Case Green Sedge.

LARVAE

Hydropsyche Larva with latex thorax.

Simple Caddis Larva (*Cheumatopsyche*).

Green Caddis (Green Rock Worm) Larva.

Peeking Caddis Larva (soft body).

Wiggle Larva (Hydropsychidae).

Peeking Caddis Larva (hard body).

Tying Instructions

With more and more anglers practicing catch-and-release, realistic flies have become necessary for success. Realistic meaning more than mere appearance but also natural action and performance. When tying caddis imitations you must consider many factors, including size, translucence, silhouette and action. You also must be aware of the type of water the fly will be fished in. Fast-water flies need more flotation and generally need not be as exact in appearance as flies to be fished in calm, glassy waters. This is true of any imitation. Following are some of the design problems and our solutions for imitations of the various stages of caddisflies.

Campodeiform Larvae

(Larvae That Do Not Build Cases
Except Just Before Pupation)

These are the free-living types, tunnelers, netspinners and roamers and include the super important netspinners, Hydropsychidae, and the true free-living worms *Rhyacophila*.

When tying non-case-building larval imitations, keep in mind two larval habits which must be incorporated into the design; 1) They drift with their heads down so they may reattach to the bottom, 2) They raise and lower themselves in the water by curling and uncurling their bodies using their anal brush for propulsion. This occurs during the "drift". The solution to the first problem is simple, tie the fly with the head at the bend of the hook. The second problem is more complicated. The solution is to construct a wiggle larva similar to the wiggle nymphs for mayflies, or use a curved shank hook which, when it moves in the current, offers the trout a view of the fly in a straight form from the top of the hook and a curled form from the side.

Simple Larva

Little Olive Caddis Larva (*Cheumatopsyche*)

Hook: *Tiemco TMC 2487, 2XS 2XW, size 14*
Body: *Green spun fur or synthetic dubbing*
Legs: *Cream soft hackle*
Head: *Black thread*
Rib: *Copper wire*
Tail: *Cream soft hackle*

1. Weight the hook by wrapping it with lead wire and secure it with tying thread.

2. Form a head of tying thread and cement.

3. Tie-in hackle and copper wire for rib. Dub a thorax.

4. Wrap the hackle.

5. Dub the body. Wrap the rib. Tie in the short tail. Whip finish and cement. Clip the hackle to leave legs on the sides and bottom of the fly and pick out fur to imitate gills.

Wiggle Larva

Cinnamon Caddis Larva (*Hydropsyche*)

Hooks: *Tiemco TMC 2487, size12*
Body: *Tan spun fur or synthetic dubbing*
Legs: *Tan soft hackle*
Head and Thorax: *Black thread and brown fur*
Rib: *Gold wire*
Tail: *Cream soft hackle*

1. Wrap the head at the bend of a curved shank hook. Dub a thorax. Tie-in a soft hackle feather for legs.

2. Tie-in the wire rib. Dub this half of the body to the hook eye and wrap the rib. Whip finish and cement. Cut the bend of the hook off near the head.

3. Lash a piece of mono to project off the back of the second curved shank hook and loop it through the eye of the front section and lash it back to the hook. Make sure that the loop is open to allow free movement. Super glue the wrapping or it may slip.

4. Tie-in the wire for the rib. Dub the back half of the body. Tie-in the short tail fibers.

5. Wrap the rib and tie-off. Pick out fur on bottom.

Exact Imitation

Cinnamon Caddis Larva (*Hydropsyche/Ceratopsyche*)

Hook: *Tiemco TMC 3761, 1XL 2X, heavy*
Body: *Gray spun fur or synthetic dubbing*
Legs: *Tan turkey tail fibers*
Head and Thorax: *Liquid latex and acrylic paint mixed*
Rib: *Clear mono thread*
Tail: *Cream soft hackle*

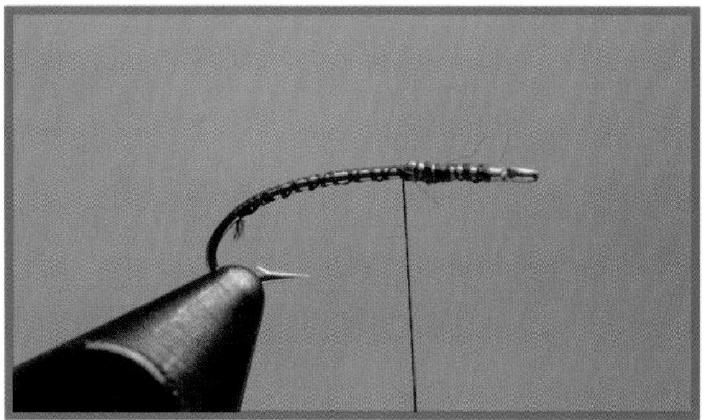

1. Tie-in two pieces of lead wire just behind the eye, on the sides of the hook, to extend to the end of the thorax area.

2. Take the thread back to a little beyond the bend of the hook, tie-in the short tail section and the ribbing.

3. Dub the abdomen to the thorax.

4. Wrap the ribbing and tie-off.

5. Paint the thorax and head sections with light tan acrylic paint mixed with liquid latex.

6. Paint in the dorsal plates with dark brown acrylic paint and liquid latex mix.

7. Attach the short legs by dipping the butts of the feather fibers in liquid latex and placing them in position.

8. Pick out the fur on the bottom of the abdomen to imitate the gills.

Green Rock Worm (*Rhyacophila*)

Hook: *Tiemco TMC 3761, 1XL 2X, heavy*
Body: *Bright green Antron yarn*
Legs: *Tan turkey tail or pheasant tail fibers*
Head and Thorax: *Liquid latex and acrylic paint mixed*
Weight: *Flat lead*
Thread: *Tan*

1. Tie-in the tails.

2. Tie-in the lead wire so the middle of the body is fatter than the ends.

3. Take the thread back to a little beyond the bend of the hook and tie-in the yarn.

4. Twist the yarn tightly and wrap it to the thorax area. These worms have deep segments in their abdomen thus the yarn is wrapped so the wraps do not, or just barely, touch. Shape the thorax and head with thread and tie-off.

5. Paint the thorax and head sections with light tan acrylic paint mixed with liquid latex. Paint in the dorsal plates with light brown acrylic paint and liquid latex mix.

6. Attach the short legs by dipping the butts of the feather fibers in liquid latex and placing them in position.

Note: If a leg on the previous two imitations comes off when fishing they can be replaced by repeating Step 5.

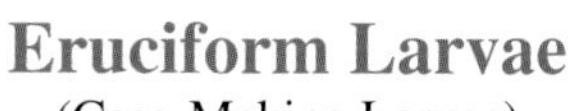

Eruciform Larvae

(Case-Making Larvae)

Studies have found that at certain seasons trout consume a huge number of case-making larvae, case and all. These larvae make up a high percentage of the trout's diet in the fall, winter and spring. This is because there is not much else to eat and the stream bottoms are devoid of aquatic vegetation which makes the larvae crawling on the substrate vulnerable. In spring and summer there are plenty of soft-bodied insects to eat and the fish probably prefer these to the hard-cased larvae.

These larvae make their cases from sand grains, pebbles and various pieces of plant life. Study the pictures of the different cases in the last part of this book and you will be able to imitate the cases of caddisflies that make cases with the two techniques we feature. Keep in mind some of these caddis larvae are small but numerous like the Grannom, and some are less numerous but very large. The very large ones are fine searching patterns and will take large trout.

Peeping Caddis (Fur Case)

Grannom (*Brachycentrus*)

Hook: *Tiemco TMC 5212, 2XL, size 14*
Case: *Spun fur from a hare's mask, guard hairs included (other fur such as muskrat, possom, beaver, etc. can be used depending on the color of the case other species' have)*
Legs: *Partridge hackle*
Head: *Antron yarn in yellow or olive*
Weight: *Lead wire*
Thread: *Brown*

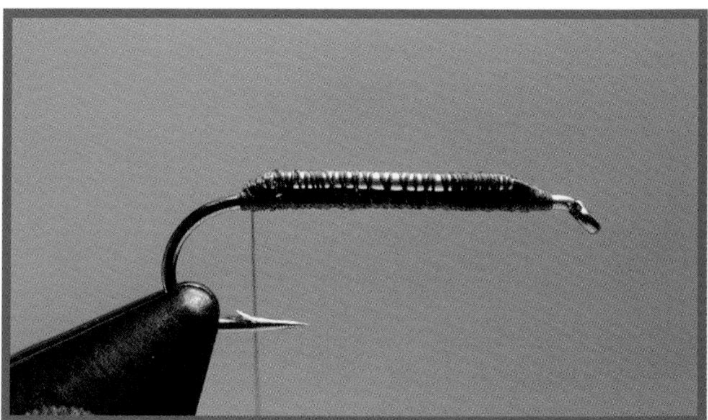

1. Weight the hook by wrapping lead wire on the hook so it is on the top of the hook.

2. Take a one-inch piece of Antron yarn and hold the end over a cigarette lighter. The fibers will fuse and turn brown. Tie-in the yarn on top of the hook at the bend so the dark head protrudes over the bend.

3. Tie-in a small partridge feather just after the yarn head and wrap two turns of hackle.

4. Use a Dubbing Loop to dub the case. It should be thick and contain the guard hairs and taper smaller back to the eye of the hook. Brush the hair out with a stiff toothbrush.

5. Clip the body to an even square taper. Some caddisflies in this family have round cases so either shape will be accurate. Check the cases in your river to see which is most common. Some families have rougher cases such as Limnephilidae. These can be left unclipped. Fur from different animals can be used for different colors.

Peeping Caddis (Hard Body)

This imitation can be tied to represent many genera which build sand and pebble cases, pebble cases and pebble and twig cases.

Hook: *Tiemco TMC 5212, 2XL, size 14*
Case: *Sand, pebbles and twigs*
Legs: *Partridge hackle*
Head: *Antron yarn in yellow or olive*
Weight: *Lead wire*
Thread: *Brown*

1. Weight the hook by wrapping it with lead wire so it is on the top of the hook.

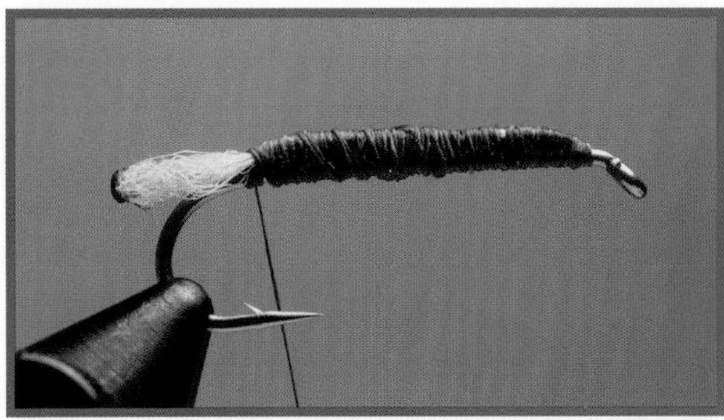

2. Take a one-inch piece of yellow or olive Antron yarn and burn the end with a cigarette lighter. The fibers will fuse and turn brown. Tie-in the yarn on top of the hook at the bend so the dark head protrudes over the bend.

3. Tie-in a small partridge feather just after the yarn head and wrap two turns of hackle.

4. Wrap an underbody of natural color dubbing.

5. Saturate the underbody with epoxy and bury the body in small pebbles, sand or a mixture of both. When the epoxy has dried, brush off the case. At this point small twigs etc. can be added for those cases which have them. See Chapter 6 for illustrations of cases to give you an idea of the forms of these naturals. Another coat of cement will make the pattern more durable.

Pupae

Pupae present a different problem. They are more complex than larvae and are available to fish in three different areas. The imitations are similar in appearance but they are fished at different depths. Trout take pupae as they drift along the bottom prior to swimming to the surface, as they swim to the surface and as they drift subsurface prior to emergence. We need three patterns, one weighted which can be drifted on the bottom with the legs in the resting position, one weighted with the middle legs fringed at the tips and projecting forward. This would be allowed to sink and then raise to the surface. The third is unweighted with the legs in the resting position to be drifted just under the surface.

Pupae

Cinnamon Caddis Pupa (*Hydropsyche/Ceratopsyche*)

Hook: *Tiemco 100, sizes 16-18, light wire*
Body: *Cinnamon spun fur or synthetic dubbing and pheasant tail fibers for those naturals with darker backs*
Legs: *Brown soft hackle*
Head: *Brown thread*
Wing Case: *Black Z-lon*
Ribbing: *Gold wire*
Antennae: *Mallard flank*

1. Tie a strand of black Z-lon on the bottom of the hook, perpendicular to the shank at a point one third of the way from the end of the hook shank. Tie-in the wire rib on the bottom of the hook.

2. Tie-in pheasant tail fibers for those flies with darker backs. Dub the body past the Z-lon to cover three quarters of the hook shank.

3. Fold the pheasant tail fibers forward and tie-in. Wrap the rib forward and tie-off.

4. Pull the Z-lon forward and tie-off on the bottom of the hook.

5. Tie-in beard-style six fibers of brown soft hackle for the legs.

6. Tie-in mono eyes or burn your own by centering an appropriate length of mono in hemos or hackle pliers and burn each end. Dub a head by figure-eighting around the eyes with dubbing. Tie-in antennae. Whip finish and cement.

Note: The fly should be weighted if you want it to sink. It should have a pair of small, fringed hackle tips for the middle legs if the swimming pupa is to be imitated. The thorax wing cases and head can be formed by painting with liquid latex and black or dark brown acrylic paint. A very realistic head, thorax and wing case can be produced by building these up in layers.

Emergers/Stillborns

Imitations of emerging caddis have far outproduced all other dry fly imitations during a hatch, especially in regards to larger, more selective fish. These are our "Don't-leave-home-without-it" flies. We believe the teardrop shaped shuck is the key because it looks just like the natural's. In a few years of fishing this fly we have not had consistently-feeding fish refuse a good presentation of it.

Bob's Teardrop Emerger

Little Olive Caddis (*Cheumatopsyche*)

Hook: *Tiemco TMC 2487, sizes 18-20*
Shuck: *Ginger Z-lon*
Body: *Green spun fur or synthetic dubbing*
Legs: *Tan hackle*
Head: *Black thread*
Wing: *Snowshoe rabbit*

1. Dub a quarter of the body from the bend of the hook.

2. Tie Z-lon so that it surrounds the hook and projects past the body by at least a sixteenth of an inch more than the body length. Tie an overhand knot around the Z-lon with a scrap of tying thread approximately three quarters the length of the body from the rear of the fly. Cut the Z-lon one sixteenth of an inch from the knot and melt it with a lighter or hot tip cauterizing tool and super glue the tip.

3. Tie-in a wing of deer hair, snowshoe rabbit hair, or poly yarn extending rearward.

4. Dub the body forward leaving room for hackle legs and head.

5. Tie-in and wrap two turns of hackle. Fold the wing forward and tie down. Trim off. Dub a small head and whip finish and cement.

Teardrop Delta Wing Emerger

This is the same as the Bob's Tear Drop Emerger except the wings are dun cock hackle tips tied-in spent and sloping back at a 45 degree angle and the hackles are omitted. It imitates a caddisfly with its wings out of the shuck and its legs stuck in the case.

Bob's Quick and Dirty Emerger

Cinnamon Sedge Emerger (*Hydropsyche/Ceratopsyche*)

Hook: *Tiemco 200R, sizes 16-22*
Thread: *The color of the body*
Shuck: *Ginger Z-lon*
Body: *Cinnamon spun fur or synthetic dubbing*
Legs: *Brown hackle*
Head: *Black thread*

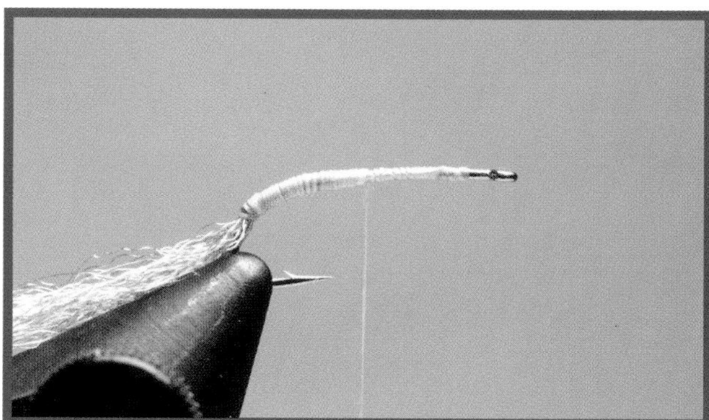

1. Tie the Z-lon extending to the rear of the hook.

2. Advance the thread one third of the hook shank forward. Dub the body to the winging point.

3. Fold the Z-lon forward and tie down, surrounding the body.

4. Tie-in and wrap two turns of hackle.

5. Tie-in a wing the length of the body on top of the hook using deer hair, poly yarn or snowshoe rabbit. Whip finish, clip the wing butts to form the head and cement the fly.

Note: These previous flies are the most important imitations in your arsenal for the emergence. Don't neglect these patterns, they are deadly when fished at the right time.

Adult Caddis

The adult is the stage which most of the previous imitations imitate. It is effective during ovipositing but lacks consistency during a hatch. The main problem imitating an adult caddis lies with the wings which are translucent and have a sheen. Hair and feathers alone do not possess this sheen. We will present some materials which overcome these difficulties.

Cinnamon Sedge Adult

(*Hydropsyche/Ceratopsyche*)

Hook: *Tiemco 100, sizes 16-18*
Body: *Cinnamon spun fur or synthetic dubbing*
Wing: *Game bird body feathers on Scotch tape*
Legs: *Brown hackle*
Head: *Black thread*
Antennae: *Brown mallard side feathers*

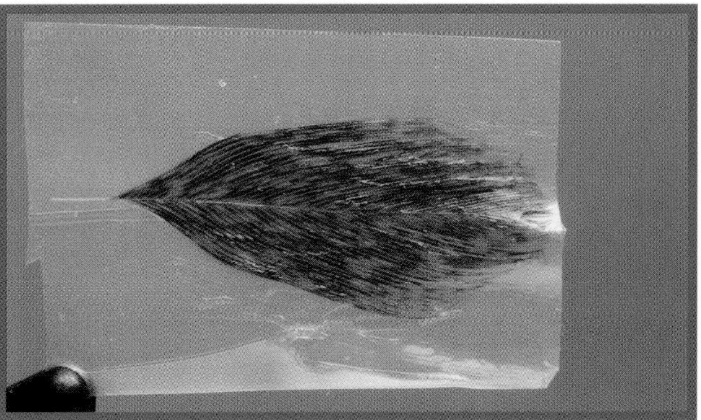

1. Preparation of the wings.
   a. Place a body feather of a Bob White, dark partridge, or ruff grouse on a piece of frosted Scotch tape.
   b. Brush Seal-All cement over the feather (the glue on the Scotch tape is not waterproof).

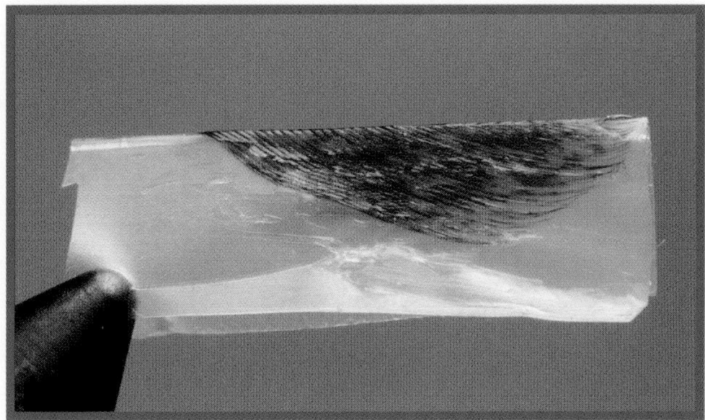

2. When the glue is dry, fold the taped feather in half at the stem.

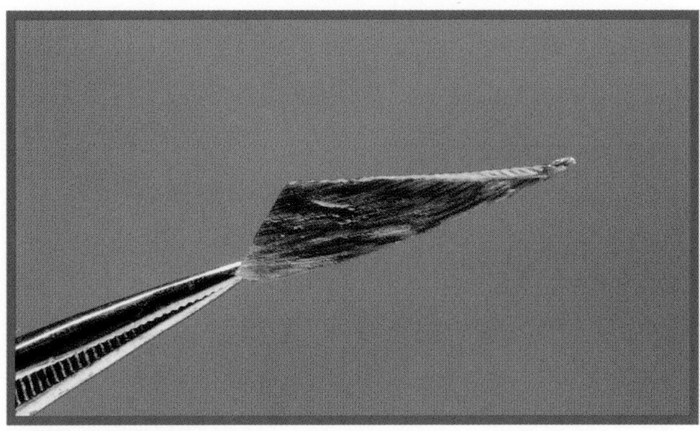

3. Clip to shape.

4. Dub a fat body.

5. Tie-in the antennae.

6. Tie-in and wrap the hackle and clip the top. You can clip the bottom when on the stream if necessary.

7. Tie-in the prepared wing and super glue the wing at the point of attachment. This keeps the wing from twisting when casting it. Tie-in the head and whip finish.

Note: When viewed from the bottom the wing needs to form an angle of 15 degrees from the outside edges. This is narrower than many patterns prescribe. If you choose to use deer hair as a wing material, you must select hair that flairs only slightly. You can narrow the angle of the wing by wrapping back up the wing three or four times with less pressure than the previous to compress it. Then wrap forward with increasing pressure to where you started. When using deer hair try placing a small amount of light dun Z-lon to add a little sheen which is present on the natural.

If you choose to use the two feather wing technique you should treat the feathers with a tough adhesive. Goop or Aqua Seal thinned with acetone or Goof Off are the best adhesives we are aware of. Apply the cement by putting a drop on the lower part of the feather and drawing it between your fingers.

A new material that looks promising is Shimzaki Air-Thru. The best way to shape this material is to fold it twice, placing it in wing burners with the bottom of the burner one sixteenth of an inch to the fold. Burn only the top of the wing with the Hot-Tip cauterizing tool. Then cut the bottom and back of the wing. This material melts and fuses the top of the wing, and by trimming the rest we can open them up so they tie-in tent-like over the body. This material takes markers and acrylic paint well so spots and patterns can be placed easily.

No matter what material is used for the wings be aware that different families of caddisflies have differently shaped wings, these are illustrated so you can match the correct shape of the insect you are imitating.

Spent Caddis

Female caddisflies die after ovipositing and once their muscles have relaxed they offer a distinct and large silhouette, and an easy meal. They are taken during the night and early in the morning. The problem with tying spent caddis is similar to tying adults, the wings need translucency and a sharp silhouette.

Quad Wing Spent Caddis

Little Olive Caddis (*Cheumatopsyche*)

Hook: *Tiemco 100, sizes 18-20*
Body: *Green spun fur or synthetic dubbing*
Wings: *Partridge body feathers*
Legs: *Tan hackle*
Head: *Black thread*

1. Dub the body two thirds up the hook shank.

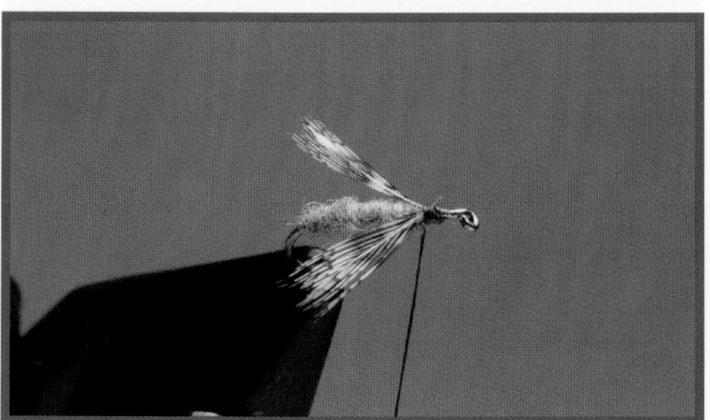

2. Tie-in two partridge feathers pointing back so that the nearest edge of the feather is close to, if not touching, the body.

3. Tie-in slightly larger wings and figure-eight around them to make them perpendicular to the hook shank.

4. Wrap three turns of dry fly hackle between the front and rear wing.

5. Wrap the head. Tie-off and cement.

Note: The Delta Wing Caddis is the same except that only two wings are tied-in and they are usually cock hackle.

Antron Spent Caddis

Hook: *Tiemco 100, sizes 18-20*
Body: *Spun fur or synthetic dubbing*
Wings: *Antron*
Legs: *Hackle*
Head: *Black thread*

1. Dub a body.

2. Tie-in Antron wings facing rearward.

3. Top view of Step 2.

4. Tie-in and wrap hackle.

5. The finished Antron Spent Caddis.

Chapter IV

CADDISFLY SUPER HATCH LISTS AND FISHERMEN'S KEYS TO CADDISFLIES

The following are lists of caddisflies that we have found to create true super hatches in each region of the country.

Our definition of a super caddis species is one which causes heavy feeding by trout over at least a one-week period. Following each super hatch list is a list of caddisflies which can cause feeding by trout and may be important in certain areas, but neither we, nor our friends, have found to be of overwhelming importance. These super hatch lists are purely subjective, they are the result of many years experience by ourselves and many others, but since nobody has fished every trout stream in the country, it is entirely possible the reader may find a caddisfly on his home stream which he considers a super caddisfly that we do not list as such. For this reason we have developed an easy, non-scientific key with which the angler can discover what genera, and often what species, is on the water he is fishing. The angler must catch a natural, note the color of the wings and body and the overall length. He can then go through the step-by-step, numbered keys to easily identify the insect. There is a diagnostic verification after each listing that the angler can use to be sure of the identification. Even though this requires the use of a microscope this verification is also simple and quick.

These keys are for trout streams and in many cases smallmouth bass streams. They are not intended for stillwaters nor for warm-water streams. Obscure families, genera and species of caddisflies, and warm-water species which trout fishermen would almost never encounter, have been eliminated for simplicity.

Once the angler has identified the insect, a chapter with complete descriptions of the family, genera and species is provided. He can look up any caddisfly he is interested in and discover the habits and a complete description of the natural.

South Holsten River rainbow.

Caddis Super Hatches of the Eastern United States

■ = Most important caddisflies
■ = Very important caddisflies
■ = Important caddisflies
■ = Occasionally important caddisflies, may be important locally

1. **Little Black Caddis,** a k a Grannom, sizes 16-18.
(Brachycentridae; *Brachycentrus numerosus, lateralis appalachia* and *solomoni*). Extremely important early spring for a few weeks with explosive daytime emergence.

2. **Spotted Sedge,** a k a Cinnamon Sedge, sizes 16-18.
(Hydropsychidae; *Hydropsyche/Ceratopsyche bronta, sparna* and *morosa*). Most important genera of all Trichoptera all season, usually evening emergence but can come in early morning, sometimes has a light morning and heavy evening emergence.

3. **Little Olive Sedge,** a k a Little Sister Sedge, sizes 20-22.
(Hydropsychidae; *Cheumatopsyche pettiti* and *harwoodi*). Second most important genera of all Trichoptera all season with a morning and evening emergence.

4. **Little Black Short-Horned Sedge,** sizes 20-22.
(Glossosomatidae; *Glossosoma nigrior*). Important early in the season in the morning, and June evenings.

5. **Dark Blue Sedge,** sizes 16-18.
(Odontoceridae; *Psilotreta labia*). Very important from New England to mid-South, from late April to June in the evening.

6. **Plain Red-Brown Long-Horned Sedge,** sizes 16-18.
(Leptoceridae; *Oecetis inconspicua*). Important mid-summer evenings.

7. **Green Sedge,** sizes 16-18.
(Rhyacophilidae; *Rhyacophila fuscula,* most common species). Important on fast cold streams from late spring to fall. Hatches sporadically in some areas.

8. **Plain Brown Long-Horned Scaly Wing Sedge,** sizes 16-18.
(Leptoceridae; *Ceraclea transversa*). Important on summer evenings.

9. **Little Grannom,** size 20.
(Brachycentridae; *Micrasema rusticum, charonis, scotti wataga*) Small, dark form, important on summer evenings in spring and fall in southern Appalachia.

10. **Dot Wing Sedge,** size 18.
(Limnephilidae; *Frenesia missa*). Very important in late fall, October-November, late morning and afternoon.

Caddis Which Are Sometimes Significant in the Eastern United States But Do Not Reach Super Hatch Status

1. **Early Smoky Wing Sedge,** sizes 20-22.
(Limnephilidae; *Apatania incerta*). Rates **very important** in southern New England early in the season.

2. **Summer Flier,** sizes 14-16.
(Limnephilidae; *Limnephilus submonilifer*).
Mostly lake species but can inhabit slower streams.

3. **Little Brown Sedge,** size 16.
(Lepidostomatidae; *Lepidostoma vernalis*).
Important in small woodland streams.

4. **Tiny Black Caddis,** sizes 20-22.
(Philopotamidae; *Chimarra aterrima*). We have not found this species important but other writers say it is.

5. **Speckled Peter,** sizes 20-22.
(Helicopsychidae; *Helicopsyche borealis*).
Very small form with brown speckled wings.

6. **Black Wing Long-Horned Sedge,** a k a Black Dancer, sizes 18-20.
(Leptoceridae; *Mystacides sepulchralis*). Daytime emerger.

7. **Brown Checkered Summer Sedge,** size 18.
(Polycentropidae, *Polycentropus cinereus*). This small, brown-checkered-wing insect is found in quiet, cool streams in summer.

8. **Dinky Light Summer Sedge,** sizes 20-22.
(Limnephilidae; *Nyctiophylax moestus*).
Small, yellow-brown species found in quiet streams.

9. **Great Brown Autumn Sedge,** size 10.
(Limnephilidae; *Pycnopsyche guttifer*). Flies mostly at night but is very large and can provide good action at dusk and after.

10. **Giant Black and Tan-Patterned Wing Sedge,** a k a Zebra Caddis, sizes 12-14.
(Hydropsychidae; *Macronema zebratum*). Can rate **most important** on smallmouth bass streams and warm trout streams like the Housatonic in Connecticut. This is a daytime emerger.

This nice rainbow fell for a caddis pupa.

11. **Microcaddis,** sizes 26-28.
(Hydroptilidae; *Hydroptila hamata*). If not overwhelmed by larger flies this insect can be important because they often hatch in great numbers.

12. **Dinky Purple-Breasted Sedge,** size 22.
(Psychomyiidae; *Psychomyia flavida*). Usually emerges after dark but can come on cloudy days.

13. **White Miller,** sizes 14-16.
(Leptoceridae; *Nectopsyche albida* and *exquisita*). Emerges at dusk and after dark.

14. **Giant Cream-Patterned Wing Sedge,** sizes 8-10.
(Limnephilidae; *Hydratophylax argus*). Can be important in Eastern streams in the morning.

15. **Chocolate and Cream Sedge,** sizes 8-10.
(Limnephilidae; *Platycentropus radiatus*).
Most activity takes place at night.

16. **Dark Eastern Woodland Sedge,** sizes 20-22.
(Psychomyiidae; *Lype diversa*).
Can be significant on small, cool woodland streams.

17. **Little Gray Sedge,** size 18.
(Limnephilidae; *Goera calcarata*).
Can be common in small, fast streams, especially common in Appalachian streams.

18. **Gray Checkered Sedge,** sizes 14-16.
(Molannidae; *Molanna cinera* and *uniophila*).
Most often found in lakes.

Caddis Super Hatches of the Midwestern United States

1. **Little Black Caddis,** a k a White Wing Black Caddis, Grannom, Popcorn Caddis, sizes 16-18.
(Brachycentridae, *Brachycentrus numerosus, lateralis* and *americanus*). Extremely important in spring. *B. lateralis* is the most important in our experience and is the big hatch on the Au Sable in Michigan. People have been incorrectly calling it *Chimarra* which is not important in our experience.

2. **Cinnamon Sedge,** a k a Spotted Sedge, sizes 16-18. (Hydropsychidae; *Ceratopsyche bifida, sparna, slossonae, recurvata, bronta* and *Hydropsyche phalerata*). Extremely important over entire season, most important genera of all Trichoptera. The genera *Hydropsyche* and *Ceratopsyche* in North America consist of approximately 70 species, the *bifida* species group (Ross, 44) was renamed genus *Symphitopsyche* (Ross and Unzicker, 77); this name is no longer valid in North America. The group was later renamed *Ceratopsyche* which is the valid term. All the species look very much alike except that many *Hydropsyche* have tan markings at the top of the wing which look like a little window in the wing.

3. **Little Olive Sedge,** a k a Little Sister Sedge, sizes 20-22. (Hydropsychidae; *Cheumatopsyche speciosa, pettiti, lasa* and *campyla*). Extremely important over entire season, this genus is a close second to *Hydropsyche* in importance.

4. **Little Black Short-Horned Sedge,** sizes 20-22. (Glossosomatidae; *Glossosoma nigrior*). Of some importance on spring mornings, important on June evenings.

5. **Green Sedge,** sizes 14-18. (Rhyacophilidae; *Rhyacophila manistee;* most common sp., *R. melita* most numerous species on Au Sable River). Important in June in the morning and evening on cold trout streams only.

6. **Yellow Sedge,** sizes 16-18. (Hydropsychidae; *Potamyia flava*). Important in late spring to early fall in the evening on large rivers in the Midwest and South.

7. **Tan Spotted Wing Long-Horned Sedge,** sizes 16-18. (Leptoceridae; *Oecetis avara*). Important in midsummer in the evening on all types of trout streams.

8. **Little Grannom,** size 20. (Brachycentridae; *Micrasema rusticum*) Important in late June and July in evening on all types of streams.

9. **Plain Brown Long-Horned Sedge,** sizes 16-18. (Leptoceridae; *Oecetis inconspicua*). Important midsummer evenings on all types of trout streams.

10. **White Miller,** a k a White Wing Long-Horned Sedge, sizes 14-16. (Leptoceridae; *Nectopsyche albida* and *exquisita*). Important summer evenings and after dark on all types of trout streams.

11. **Small Dot Wing Sedge,** sizes 18-20. (Uenoidae (this family used to be in Limnephilidae); *Neophylax fuscous*). Very important in September and October on Midwestern rivers in the daytime with large hatches and heavy feeding.

Caddis Which Are Sometimes Significant In The Midwest But Do Not Reach Super Hatch Status

1. **Tiny Black Caddis,** sizes 20-22. (Philopotamidae; *Chimarra aterrima*). Has been called important in spring but we have not seen this.

2. **Gold Speckled Wing Caddis,** size 20. (Philopotamidae; *Dolophilodes distinctus*). Wingless females in winter and spring, wings present in summer. Small, dark form. Emergence is sparse but relentless. Seems to emerge sparsely every day in spring and summer. If you see trout feeding every once in a while, but can't see anything in the water, it's a good bet they are taking this insect.

3. **Black Wing Long-Horned Sedge,** a k a Black Dancer, sizes 18-20. (Leptoceridae; *Mystacides sepulchralis*). Can produce rises in spring and early summer. Mad River in Ohio has large daytime hatches in April.

4. **Dark Woodland Sedge,** sizes 20-22. (Psychomyiidae; *Lype diversa*). Can be important on small, cool, woodland streams.

5. **Summer Flier Sedge,** sizes 14-16. (Limnephilidae; *Limnephilus sericus, moestus, submonilifer*). Most species are lake species but can inhabit slower stretches of streams.

6. **Brown Scaly Wing Sedge,** sizes 16-18. (Leptoceridae; *Ceraclea arielles, transversa*). Rates **important** for late evening and night fishermen.

7. **Giant Black and Tan-Patterned Wing Sedge,** a k a Zebra Caddis, sizes 12-14. (Hydropsychidae; *Macronema zebratum*). Rates for large, warmer trout streams and **most important** for smallmouth bass streams.

8. **Little Brown Sedge,** size 18. (Lepidostomadae; *Lepidostomata togatum*). Rates **very important** for small, cool woodland streams.

9. **Gray Checkered Sedge,** size 14.
(Molannidae; *Molanna uniophila*).
Most often found in lakes.

10. **Rush Sedge,** sizes 8-10.
(Phryganeidae; *Phryganea cinnera*).
These large gray, brown and yellow patterned winged insects can be important on some rivers in late spring and early summer.

11. **Giant Cream-Patterned Wing Sedge,** sizes 8-10.
(Limnephilidae; *Hydratophylax argus*). Large light brown with cream-patterned wing, can be important in Eastern streams in the morning in June and July.

12. **Great Brown Autumn Sedge,** sizes 8-10.
(Limnephilidae; *Pycnopsyche lipida* and *guttifer*). Fly mostly at night with some late evening and early morning spillover. This can be very important in Michigan on the Muskegon and other Midwestern rivers in October.

13. **Silver Striped Sedge,** sizes 8-10.
(Limnephilidae; *Hesperophylax designatus*).
Emerge at night.

14. **Autumn Mottled Sedge,** size 18, second species sizes 14-16.
(Limnephilidae; *Neophylax autumnus=concinnus*).
These can be important in fall when few other insects are hatching.

15. **Little Gray Sedge,** size 18.
(Limnephilidae; *Goera stylata*).
Can be common in small fast streams, is especially common in Appalachian streams.

16. **True Microcaddis and *Pseudo* Microcaddis,** sizes 24-36.
(Hydroptilidae sp. and *Pseudo* Microcaddis; (Glossosomatidae; *Protoptila* sp.). Can rate **very important** if not overwhelmed by larger species because they often emerge in large numbers.

17. **Giant Rusty Sedge,** sizes 10-12.
(Phryganeidae; *Ptilostomis ocellifera* and *semifasciata*). Rates **very important** for night fishermen in summer.

18. **Golden Wing Dancer,** sizes 18-20.
(Leptoceridae; *Mystacides interjecta*). Long-horned sedge.

19. **Brown Checkered Summer Sedge,** sizes 18-20.
(Polycentropidae; *Polycentropus cinereus*).
This small brown checkered wing caddisfly is found in quiet, cool streams in summer.

20. **Dinky Light Summer Sedge,** sizes 22-24.
(Polycentropidae; *Nyctiophylax moestus*).
This small species is yellowish-brown and is found on quiet streams.

21. **Chocolate and Cream Sedge,** sizes 12-14.
(Limnephilidae; *Platycentropus radiatus*).
Most feeding takes place at night but this is a large insect.

22. **Speckled Peter,** sizes 20-22.
(Helicopsychidae; *Helicopsyche borealis*).
This tiny caddisfly with brown speckled wings is most abundant in slower currents.

Caddis Super Hatches of the Western United States

1. **Little Black Caddis,** a k a Grannom, Mother's Day Caddis, sizes 16-18.
(Brachycentridae; *Brachycentrus occidentalis* and *americanus*). *B. occidentalis* is very important for a short time in spring, usually before runoff in the daytime; *B. americanus* has a longer, less explosive emergence in the morning in midsummer.

2. **Spotted Sedge,** a k a Cinnamon Sedge, sizes 16-18.
(Hydropsychidae; *Hydropsyche cockerlli, occidentalis, oslara* and *placoda*). Most important family of all Trichoptera by a wide margin during the entire season; and most important genus, usually evening emergence but can come in the morning.

3. **Little Summer Olive Sedge,** a k a Little Sister Sedge, sizes 18-22.
(Hydropsychidae; *Cheumatopsyche pettiti, lassa* and *campyla*). Second most important genus of all Trichoptera all season, morning and evening emergence.

Bighorn brown.

4. **Little Black Short-Horned Sedge,** sizes 20-24.
(Glossosomatidae; *Glossosoma montana*). Important late May to September at times, emergence in the evening.

5. **Gray Wing Long-Horned Sedge**, sizes 16-18.
(Leptoceridae; *Oecetis disjuncta*). Important late June at peak emergence late afternoon and evenings.

6. **Speckled Peter,** sizes 20-22.
(Helicopsychidae; *Helicopsyche borealis)*.
Important Mid-June to early July; very small form.

7. **Tan Spotted Wing Long-Horned Sedge,** sizes 16-18.
(Leptoceridae; *Oecetis avara*).
Important at mid-July peak emergence.

8. **Little Brown Sedge,** size 18.
(Lepidostomatidae; *Lepidostomata pluviale*).
Important mid-June to late September at times of peak emergence, from small, cool streams.

9. **Little Grannom**, sizes 20-22.
(Brachycentridae; *Micrasema bactro* and *Amiocentrus aspilis*).
Important in late June in the evening on the Yellowstone, the latter spring and August and September on the Bighorn.

10. **Black Wing Long-Horned Sedge**, a k a Black Dancer, size 16.
(Leptoceridae; *Mystacides alafimbriata*). Very important late June to early July in the morning and evening.

11. **Green Sedge**, sizes 14-18.
(Rhyacophilidae; *Rhyacophila grandus, bifila, coloradensis*). Can be important on fast rivers but often emerges sporadically.

12. **Giant Orange Sedge,** sizes 4-8.
(Limnephilidae; *Dicosmoecus atripes, gilvipes* and *jucundus*). Extremely important on Pacific Coast rivers and the Missouri in Montana in fall in the afternoon and evening.

Caddis Which Are Sometimes Significant In The Western United States But Do Not Reach Super Hatch Status

1. **Great Gray Spotted Sedge,** sizes 8-10.
(Hydropsychidae; *Arctopsyche grandus*).
Emerges at night but is large and makes a good searching pattern. Body is bright olive to brownish-olive depending on the river. Wings are grayish-brown with lighter brown speckles, legs are brown and antennae are brown with darker rings. Length is 17-20mm.

2. **Microcaddis sp.,** sizes 24-28.
(Hydroptilidae; *Agraylea, Hydroptila, Leucotrichia, Oxyethira,* sp.). Can be very important at times if not overshadowed by larger species. Can be just about any color. These tiny caddisflies often emerge in huge numbers and at times fish feed selectively on them. Good imitations of pupae, emergers and adults are necessary even though these caddisflies are very small.

3. **Autumn Mottled Sedge,** sizes 12-14.
(Limnephilidae; *Neophylax rickeri* and *splendens*).
Body is brownish-yellow, wings are mottled brown, 16-18mm. These caddisflies are very important in the Pacific Northwest and although present in the Rocky Mountain states are not as numerous. They emerge from the faster riffles in midstream. Egg-laying is on objects near the stream so this stage is not important to fishermen. Emergence is from September to October and well coordinated in a three-week period.

4. **Tiny Purple Breasted Sedge,** sizes 20-22.
(Psychomyiidae; *Psychomyia flavida*).
Usually emerges after dark but can come on cloudy days. Very small insects, 5-6mm, body is yellow with a purple tinge, wings and legs are brown. These insects are most abundant in faster sections of large and small streams and emerge midsummer.

5. **Silver Striped Sedge,** sizes 8-10.
(Limnephilidae; *Hesperophylax designatus, incisis*).
These large caddisflies, up to 34mm, emerge after dark in midsummer. The wings are cream and light brown patterned with a silver stripe, body and legs are straw colored.

6. **Great Autumn Mottled Sedge,** sizes 8-10.
(Limnephilidae; *Pycnopsyche guttifer*).
These very large caddisflies are uncommon in the West but the Bighorn River in Montana has a good hatch in September. Emergence is at dusk and after dark.

7. **Cinnamon Autumn Sedge,** sizes 8-10.
(Limnephilidae; *Limnephilus thorus*).
These large caddisflies are found on the Bighorn River in Montana. We collected this species in late September 1995 for a two-week period near Camp Cottonwood below the Yellow Tail Dam. We sent them to Dr. Brian Armatige, director of the Ohio Biological Survey for identification. He reported them a new find for Montana. Since the Bighorn is one of, if not, the best trout streams in the country we include the species here. They are present in some other Western states. The emergence occurs in large numbers in the evening from midstream. Egg-laying is on objects near the stream.

Fishermen's Key to Eastern Caddisflies

■ = Most important caddisflies

■ = Very important caddisflies

■ = Important caddisflies

■ = Occasionally important caddisflies, may be important locally

* Beginning of peak activity.

** "Notes" begin on page 47.

Note: These keys only apply to caddis found on trout streams in sufficient enough numbers to cause selective trout feeding.

Note: Bold data is all that is needed for determination.

ADULTS	
1. Size from head to wing tips usually less than 5mm, usually 1-4mm, very hairy, fig. 1	11
2. Size less than 6mm, not hairy, fig. 2	12
3. Size from head to wing tips 5.5mm to 8mm	13
4. Antennae more than twice the length of body, fig. 3	14
5. Antennae less than twice the length of body, fig. 4	6-10
6. Size 8-14mm, body black or dark gray	15
7. Size 8-14mm, body olive or olive brown	16
8. Size 8-14mm, body yellow to medium brown	17
9. Size 13mm to 20mm	18
10. Size 21mm to 34mm	19

11. True Microcaddis (Family Hydroptilidae), **very hairy, unique wing shape (see figure 1)**.

a. **Body brown, legs dark brown, very dark brown to black with a few scattered light spots, white bands around the antennae, 3-4.5mm,** late June and early July, E M W. **(Ring-Horned Microcaddis)** Hydroptilidae; *Leucotrichia pictipes.*

b. **Body green, wings speckled gray and white, legs very dark brown, 3-4.5mm,** May to July, hatch widespread, important species, E M W. **(Salt and Pepper Microcaddis)** Hydroptilidae; *Agraylea multipunctata.*

c. **Body light greenish-yellow, wings, cream and brown mottled, legs light yellow, 2-3mm,** May to October, E M W. **(Cream and Brown Mottled Microcaddis)** Hydroptilidae; *Oxyethira serrata, pallida, michiganensis.*

d. **Body bright yellow, orange-brown and shades in between, wings gray to brown, can be solid or spotted, legs yellow to black, 2.5-4mm,** spring to fall **(Vari-Colored Microcaddis)** three important species W, *H. acoma, rono, argosa*, three species E M W, *H. ajax, hamata, consimilis*, three species E M, *H. jack manni, albicornis, waubesiana.* Color and size can vary even in the same species.

Bighorn River in the evening.

e. **Color other than a. b. c. d.** Hydroptilidae; *Hydroptila* sp.

12. a. Colors **variable, 3-5.5mm, (*Pseudo* Microcaddis)** Glossosomatidae; *Protoptila* sp. Not hairy.

13. a. **Body very dark brown almost black, sides of abdomen white, wing black, 6-8mm,** emergence early May* **(Tiny Black Caddis)** Philopotamidae; *Chimarra aterrima, socia.* (See Note A for diagnostic verification).**

b. **Body amber to yellow, wings light brown with heavy speckling of dark brown, 5.5-7mm,** emergence mid-May* **(Speckled Peter)** Helicopsychidae; *Helicopsyche borealis.* (See Note B for diagnostic verification).**

c. **Body dark brown, wings dark gray, 6-7mm,** emergence mid-June* **(Dark Eastern Woodland Sedge)** Psychomyiidae; *Lype diversa.* (See Note C for diagnostic verification).**

d. **Body and wings yellowish-brown, wings brown, 5-7mm,** June and July **(Dinky Light Summer Sedge)** Polycentropodidae; *Nyctiophylax moestus.* (See Note I for diagnostic verification).**

e. **Body smoky brown, wings smoky gray, 7-8.5mm,** mid-April to late May **(Early Smoky Wing Sedge)** Limnephilidae; *Apatania incerta.* (See Note K for diagnostic verification).**

f. **Body, wings and appendages grayish-black, 6-7.5mm,** emergence Mid-May to late June **(Little Black Short-Horned Sedge)** Glossosomatidae; *Glossosoma nigrior* (See Note D for diagnostic verification).**

g. **Body, wings and appendages very dark brown, almost black, 6-7.5mm,** emergence mid-May through July **(Little Grannom)** Brachycentridae; *Micrasema rusticum, charonis, scotti wataga.* (See Note E for diagnostic verification).**

14. a. **Body black, wings black, wing type C,** fig. 2, **8-9mm,** emergence mid-July* **(Black Dancer)** Leptoceridae; *Mystacides sepulchralis.*

b. **Body and wings yellow to brown, wing type C,** 10-12mm, emergence late May to mid-August **(Long-Horned Sedge)** Leptoceridae; *Oecetis inconspicua, avara, cinereus, osteni.*

c. **Body and wings dark brown or dark gray, wings often have white patches of hair or scales, wing type C,** midsummer emergence, 11-13mm, **(Scaly Wing Long-Horned Sedge)** Leptoceridae; *Ceraclea transversa* most common sp. (See key to the genera of Leptoceridae for diagnostic verification).

d. **Body light green with ginger thorax, wing cream with some tan markings, wing type C,** emerges late July to second week of September, 14-16mm, **(White Miller)** Leptoceridae; *Nectopsyche, albida, exquisita, diarana.*

e. **Body black with light rings, wings shiny black with distinctive tannish-yellow pattern, emerges early to late August, (Black and Tan-Patterned Wing Sedge),** 15-18mm, Hydropsychidae; *Macronema zebratum.*

15. a. **Body dusky brownish-gray almost black, with green or tan lateral line, wings tawny with a series of pale spots, legs and antennae paler than body, males 8-10mm, females 11-12.5mm,** mid-April to last of May, **(Little Black Caddis, a k a American Grannom)** Brachycentridae; *Brachycentrus numerosus.* (See Note F for diagnostic verification of genus).**

b. **Body, males very similar to *B. numerosus*, 6-8mm, females slightly lighter, 9-11mm, wings pale gray with a slightly darker anterior margin,** first of May to end of May, earlier in the South **(Little Black Caddis, a k a Grannom)** Brachycentridae; *Brachycentrus lateralis.* (See Note F for diagnostic verification of genus).**

c. **Males appendages fuscous, legs paler, wings fuscous with pale spots, 7-8mm; females, body straw colored, head and thorax dorosomesally darkened with brownish tinge, wings pale gray, 8-10mm,** emergence April in Georgia and May further north **(Grannom, a k a Little Black Caddis)** Brachycentridae; *Brachycentrus appalachia.* (See Note F for diagnostic verification of genus).**

d. **Body fuscous, tibia and tarsi paler, wings fuscous with paler spots in an indistinct subapical band, emergence mid-April to mid-May, males 9-10mm, females 11-13mm, (Grannom)** Brachycentridae; *Brachycentrus solomoni.* (See Note F for diagnostic verification of genus).**

e. **Body dark gray with tan lateral line, wings dark brown with light tan dots, legs brown, 9-12mm,** last of August to October **(Small Dot Wing Sedge)** Limnephilidae **(now Uenoidae)**; *Neophylax fuscus.* (See Notes M and Q for diagnostic verification).**

16. a. **Body olive, wing light to dark grayish-brown, usually with some tan or cream mottling, wing type D, 7-11mm,** emergence early May to September **(Little Summer Olive Sedge, a k a Little Sister Sedge)** Hydropsychidae; *Cheumatopsyche pettiti, harwoodi.* (See Note G for diagnostic verification).**

b. **Body olive green, wing gray mottled with brown spots, 8-16mm,** emergence May 25 to August 15 **(Green Sedge)** Rhyacophiladae; *Rhyacophila fuscula, vuphipes*, 15-18mm. (See Note H for diagnostic verification of genus).**

c. **Body green, wings dark grayish-brown with very small, irregularly scattered light spots, 12-14mm,** late May to mid-June **(Dark Blue Sedge)** Odontoceridae; *Psilotreta labia.* (See Note P for diagnostic verification).**

17. a. **Body yellowish-brown, wings light and dark brown checkered, 7-9mm,** early June to mid-July **(Brown Checkered Summer Sedge)** Polycentropodidae; *Polycentropus cinereus.* (See Note I for diagnostic verification).**

b. **Body brownish-gray, wings brown with extensive pale spots, males 7-10mm, females 11-13mm,** emergence mid-May to mid-July **(American Grannom)** Brachycentridae; *Brachycentrus americanus.* (See Note F for diagnostic verification of genus).**

c. **Body shades of brown, wings grayish-brown with a mottled pattern of lighter brown, wing type D, 8-11mm.** Most *Hydropsyche* have tan marks on the top of the wing which look like a little window in the wing when viewed from the top. This is the old *Scalaris* group. *Ceratopsyche* are the Spotted Sedge or Cinnamon Caddis, this is the old *bifila* group of

Hydropsyche. Emergence second week in May to late August **(Spotted Sedge and Window Wing Sedge)** Hydropsychidae; *Ceratopsyche morosa, sossonae, bronta, bifila, sparna, recurvata; Hydropsyche simulans, vexa, bentteni, bidens, phalerata.* (See Note J for diagnostic verification).**

d. **Body yellow, wings gray, 8-10mm,** emergence last week of May **(Little Gray Sedge)** Limnephilidae; *Goera stylata.* (See Note K for diagnostic verification).**

e. **Body yellowish-olive to tan, wings an even light brown and brown, 9-11mm,** emergence first of June **(Little Plain Brown Sedge)** Lepidostomatidae; *Lepidostoma togatum.* (See Note L for diagnostic verification).**

f. **Body brownish-yellow, wings mottled brown with a light double diamond design on top when wings are folded, legs yellowish-brown, 9-12mm,** last of September, October **(Autumn Sedge)** Limnephilidae (now Uenoidae); *Neophylax concinnus=autumnus.* (See Notes M and Q for diagnostic verification).**

18. a. **Body brown and slender with a darker dorsum, wings brown, 13-16mm,** emergence mid-April to October **(Summer Flier)** Limnephilidae; *Limnephilus submonilifer, sericus, indivisus.* (See Note K for diagnostic verification).**

b. **Body brown, wing mottled gray with checkered pattern, 14-16mm,** emergence mid-May to end of August **(Gray Checkered Sedge)** Molannidae; *Molanna uniophila* and *tryphena.* (See Note N for diagnostic verification).**

c. **Body ginger, wing yellow with brown shading, 15-18mm,** emergence mid-July to October **(Great Brown Autumn Sedge)** Limnephilidae; *Pycnopsyche lepida, guttifer.* (See Note K for diagnostic verification).**

d. **Body dark grayish-brown with yellowish-olive lateral line, wing medium brown covered with translucent tan dots, legs yellow, 11-15.5mm,** late September to November (Dot Wing Sedge) Limnephilidae; *Frenesia difficilis* (14-15.5mm) and *missa* (11.5-13.5mm). (See Note K for diagnostic verification).**

19. a. **Body dark yellow to brown, wing cream and chocolate, 20-23mm,** emergence midsummer at night **(Chocolate and Cream Sedge)** Limnephilidae; *Platycentropus radiatus.* (See Note K for diagnostic verification).**

b. **Body ginger, wings light brown and cream with "Z" pattern on wing, 28-34mm,** midsummer emerger **(Giant Cream Patterned Wing Sedge)** Limnephilidae; *Hydratophylax argus.* (See Note K for diagnostic verification).**

Fishermen's Key to Midwestern Caddisflies

■ = Most important caddisflies
■ = Very important caddisflies
■ = Important caddisflies
■ = Occasionally important caddisflies, may be important locally

* Beginning of peak activity.
** "Notes" begin on page 47.
Note: These keys only apply to caddis found on trout streams in sufficient enough numbers to cause selective trout feeding.
Note: Bold data is all that is needed for determination.

ADULTS	
1. Size from head to wing tips usually less than 5mm, usually 1-4mm, very hairy, unique wing shape, fig. 1	11
2. Size from head to wing tips less than 5.5mm, not hairy, fig. 2	12
3. Size 5.5-8mm	13
4. Antennae more than twice the length of body, fig. 3	14
5. Antennae less than twice the length of body, fig. 4, size 8mm to 13mm	6 to 8
6. Body very dark gray with a green or tan lateral line	15
7. Body olive or green	16
8. Body straw yellow to shades of brown	17
9. Antennae less than twice the length of body, size 13-20mm	18
10. Antennae less than twice the length of body, size 21-34mm	19

11. True Microcaddis (Family Hydroptilidae)

a. **Body brown, legs dark brown, very dark brown to black with a few scattered light spots, white bands around the antennae, 3-4.5mm,** late June and early July E M W **(Ring-Horned Microcaddis)**. Hydroptilidae; *Leucotrichia pictipes.*

b. **Body green, wings speckled gray and white, legs very dark brown, 3-4.5mm,** May to July hatch widespread, important species, E M W **(Salt and Pepper Microcaddis)**. Hydroptilidae; *Agraylea multipunctata.*

c. **Body light greenish-yellow, wings cream and brown mottled, legs light yellow, 2-3mm,** May to October, E M W **(Cream and Brown Mottled Microcaddis)**. Hydroptilidae; *Oxyethira serrata, pallida, michiganensis.*

d. **Body bright yellow, orange brown and shades in between, wings gray to brown, can be solid or spotted, legs yellow to black, 2.5-4mm,** spring to fall **(Vari-Colored Microcaddis)**. Three important

species W, *H. acoma, rono, argosa*, three species E M W, *H. ajax, hamata, consimilis*, three species E M, *H. jackmanni, albicornis, waubesiana.* Color and size can vary even in the same species.

e. **Color other than a. b. c. d.** Hydroptilidae; *Hydroptila* species.

12. a. **Body cinnamon, wings gray, legs cinnamon, 3-5.5mm (*Pseudo* Microcaddis, Cinnamon Caddis)** emergence August on Muskegon River. Glossosomatidae; *Protoptila immaculata.*

b. **Body and wings other colors.** Other *Protoptila* sp. A common color is black on bodies and wings.

13. a. **Body very dark brown, almost black, sides of abdomen white, wing very dark brown, 6-8mm,** emergence early May* **(Tiny Black Caddis)** Philopotamidae; *Chimarra aterrima, obscura.* (See Note A for diagnostic verification).**

b. **Body very dark brown, almost black, wings very dark brownish-gray with small gold spots, 8mm,** emergence year-round, females wingless in winter and early spring **(Small Black Gold Spotted Caddis)** Philopotamidae; *Dolophilodes distinctus.* (See Note A for diagnostic verification).**

c. **Body amber, wings light brown with heavy speckling of dark brown, 5.5-7mm,** emergence mid-May* **(Speckled Peter)** Helicopsychidae; *Helicopsyche borealis.* (See Note B for diagnostic verification).**

d. **Body black, wings dark brown, 6-7mm** emergence mid-June* **(Dark Eastern Woodland Sedge)** Psychomyiidae; *Lype diversa.* (See Note C for diagnostic verification).**

e. **Body and appendages grayish-black, wings brownish-gray with scattered gold hairs and sometimes a few scattered light spots, 5-7mm, emergence late April to late June (Little Black Short-Horned Sedge)** Glossosomatidae; *Glossosoma nigrior.* (See Note D for diagnostic verification).**

f. **Body, wings and appendages very dark brown seeming black in life, 6-7.5mm, emergence mid-May (Little Grannom)** Brachycentridae; *Micrasema rusticum.* (See Note E for diagnostic verification).**

14. a. **Body and wings shiny blue-black, wings and thorax with a metallic sheen, wing type C, 8-11mm,** emergence mid-July **(Black Dancer)** Leptoceridae; *Mystacides sepulchralis.*

b. **Body and wings rusty brown, wings cloaked in golden hairs arranged to form golden and brown bands, 8-9mm,** emergence mid-June to late August from lakes and slow-moving rivers, wing type C, **(Golden Brown Dancer)** Leptoceridae; *Mystacides longicornis.*

c. **Body yellowish-olive to tan, wing brown, wing type C,** emergence late May to mid-August, 10-12mm, **(Long-Horned Sedge)** Leptoceridae; *Oecetis* sp. **Forewings with numerous dark brown spots. Wings reddish-brown with no distinct markings** *O. inconspicua.*

d. **Body and wings vary from red-brown to brown to black, length varies from 6 to 15mm, wings often have white patches of hair or scales, wing type C,** spring to midsummer emergence **(Scaly Wing Sedge)** Leptoceridae; *Ceraclea* species. Body, wings, legs and antennae, varying shades of brown from bright reddish-brown, lighter or darker shades of brown (Brown Long-Horned Sedge) Leptoceridae; *Ceraclea transversus.* (See key to the genera of Leptoceridae for diagnostic verification).

e. **Body light green with ginger thorax, wing cream with some tan markings, wing type C,** emerges late July to second week of September, 14-16mm **(White Miller)** Leptoceridae; *Nectopsyche albida, exquisita, pavida.*

f. **Body black with light rings, wings shiny black with distinctive tannish-yellow pattern,** wing type D, emerges early to late August **(Black and Tan-Patterned Wing Sedge, a k a Zebra Caddis)**, 15-18mm, Hydropsychidae; *Macronema zebratum.*

15. a. **Body dusky brownish-gray, almost black, with a wide green lateral line in freshly-hatched adults, wings tawny with a series of pale spots, legs and antennae paler than body, males 8-10mm, females 11-12.5mm,** emergence early May* with explosive numbers **(Little Black Caddis)** Brachycentridae; *Brachycentrus numerosus* (See Note F for diagnostic verification for genus *Brachycentrus*).**

b. **Male's body and wings very similar to *B. numerosus* but smaller, 6-8mm, female's body lighter than male's, wings pale gray with a slightly darker anterior margin, 9-11mm,** emergence late April to mid-May in huge numbers **(Little Black Caddis, a k a American Grannom)** Brachycentridae; *Brachycentrus lateralis.*

c. **Body dark brownish-gray, with yellowish lateral line, wings dark grayish-brown with uniform small tan dots, legs and antennae dark straw colored, 9-11mm, emergence in fall in daytime in large numbers from September and October (Small Dot Wing Sedge)** Uenoidae; *Neophylax fuscous.* (See Note K for diagnostic verification for family Limnephilidae).** This insect is in the Uenoidae family, but keys better to Note K.

16. a. **Body olive, wing light to dark grayish-brown usually with tan and cream mottling, wing type D, 7-10mm,** emergence late April to October **(Little Sister Sedge, a k a Little Green Caddis)** Hydropsychidae; *Cheumatopsyche analis=pettiti, campyla, gracilus, speciosa, oxa.* (See Note G for diagnostic verification).**
   b. **Body olive green, wings gray mottled with brown spots, 11-13mm,** emergence May 25 to August 15 **(Green Sedge)** Rhyacophilidae; *Rhyacophila manistee* and other sp. (See Note H for diagnostic verification).**
   c. **Body green, wings dark grayish-brown with two black spots in the middle** (some other species have patches of light hair and some may have tan or brown bodies), 9-10mm, emergence first of June* **(Little Brown Sedge)** Lepidostomatidae; *Lepidostoma togatum.* (See Note L for diagnostic verification).**

17. a. **Body straw yellow, wings reddish-brown, 7-9mm,** emergence spread out, **(Little Red Twilight Sedge)** Polycentropodidae; *Neureclipsis crepuscularis.* (See Note I for diagnostic verification).**
   b. **Body brown, wings brownish with extensive pale flecks, especially around apex, males 7-10mm, females 11-13mm,** emergence late May, early July **(American Grannom)** Brachycentridae; *Brachycentrus americanus.* (See Note F for diagnostic verification for genus *Brachycentrus*).**
   c. **Body cinnamon brown, this can vary from very light (almost yellow) to darker depending on river and time of emergence, wings grayish-brown with a mottled pattern of lighter brown** (*Hydropsyche*), **or mottled shades of brown with tan mark at top of the wings (*Ceratopsyche*), wing type D, fig. 12, 8-12mm,** emergence second week in May to late August **(Cinnamon Sedge, a k a Spotted Sedge, Window Wing Sedge)** Hydropsychidae; *Ceratopsyche sparna, bifila, slossonae, bronta. Hydropsyche phalerata.* (See Note J for diagnostic verification).**
   d. **Body yellow, wings gray, 8-10mm,** emergence late May to early June **(Little Gray Sedge)** Limnephilidae; *Goera stylata.* (See Note K for diagnostic verification for Family Limnephilidae).**
   e. **Body brownish-yellow, wings mottled brown with a light double diamond design on top when wings are folded,** fig. 15, legs yellowish-brown, 9-12mm, last of September, October **(Autumn Mottled Sedge)** Limnephilidae (now Uenoidae); *Neophylax concinnus=autumnus.* (See Note K for diagnostic verification even though its family Uenoidae keys better to Limnephilidae).**
   f. **Body and wings light brownish-yellow with a pinkish cast, 10-11mm, wing type D,** May through September **(Yellow Summer Sedge)** Hydropsychidae; *Potamyia flava.* (See Note M for diagnostic verification).**

18. a. **Body reddish-brown and slender with darker dorsum, wing brown variegated with irregular light and darker spots, 13-16mm,** emergence spring to summer **(Summer Flier)** Limnephilidae; *Limnephilus sericus, submonilifer.* (See Note K for diagnostic verification for Family Limnephilidae).**
   b. **Body brown, wing mottled gray with checkered pattern, 14-16mm,** emergence mid-May to end of August **(Gray Checkered Sedge).** Molannidae; *Molanna uniophila, tryphena.* (See Note N for diagnostic verification).**
   c. **Body very dark gray to brown, wings brown with small tan translucent dots, legs yellowish-brown, 13-14mm, emergence October to December (Dot Wing Sedge)** Limnephilidae; *Frenesia missa.* (See Note K for diagnostic verification of Family Limnephilidae).**

19. a. **Body ginger, wing yellow to brown with two dark brown marks in the middle and very dark brown border at apex, 19-22mm,** emergence mid-July to October **(Great Brown Autumn Sedge)** Limnephilidae; *Pycnopsyche lepida, guttifer.* (See Note K for diagnostic verification for Family Limnephilidae).**
   b. **Body dark yellow to brown, wing cream and chocolate, 20-23mm,** emergence midsummer at night **(Chocolate and Cream Sedge)** Limnephilidae; *Platycentropus radiatus.* (See Note K for diagnostic verification for Family Limnephilidae).**
   c. **Body ginger, wings light brown and cream with "Z" pattern on wing, 28-34mm,** midsummer emerger **(Giant Cream-Patterned Wing Sedge)** Limnephilidae; *Hydratophylax argus.* (See Note K for diagnostic verification for Family Limnephilidae).**
   d. **Body reddish-brown, wing patterned gray, brown and yellow, gray patches on posterior margin form triangular plates when wings are folded, 21-25mm,** emergence last week in June to end of August **(Rush Sedge)** Phryganeidae; *Phryganea cinerea.* (See Note O for diagnostic verification).**
   e. **Body yellowish-brown, wings plain light reddish-brown, legs brown, 21-25mm,** emergence June and July after dark from lakes and slow, weedy streams **(Giant Rusty Sedge).** Phryganeidae; *Phryganea ocellifera* and *semifasciata.* (See Note O for diagnostic verification).**

Fishermen's Key to Western Caddisflies

■ = Most important caddisflies

■ = Very important caddisflies

■ = Important caddisflies

■ = Occasionally important caddisflies, may be important locally

* Beginning of peak activity.

** "Notes" begin on page 47.

Note: These keys only apply to caddis found on trout streams in sufficient enough numbers to cause selective trout feeding.

Note: Bold data is all that is needed for determination.

ADULTS	
1. Size from head to wing tips usually less than 5mm, usually 1-4mm, very hairy	10
2. Size from head to wing tips 4-7.5mm, not hairy	11
3. Antennae more than twice the length of body	12
4. Antennae less than twice the length body	5-9
5. Size 8mm to 14mm	8-9
6. Size 12mm to 16mm	15
7. Size 17mm to 34mm	16
8. Body olive or grayish-black with green lateral line	13
9. Body yellow to dark brown	14

10. True Microcaddis. Family Hydroptilidae. **Very hairy, unique wing shape (see illustration)**.
   a. **Body brown, legs dark brown, very dark brown to black with a few scattered light spots, white bands around the antennae, 3-4.5mm,** late June and early July **(Ring-Horned Microcaddis)** Hydroptilidae; *Leucotrichia pictipes.*
   b. **Body green, wings speckled gray and white, legs very dark brown, 3-4.5mm,** May to July hatch widespread, important species, **(Salt and Pepper Miocrocaddis)** Hydroptilidae; *Agraylea multipunctata.*
   c. **Body light greenish-yellow, wings cream and brown mottled, legs light yellow, 2-3mm,** May to October **(Cream and Brown Mottled Microcaddis)** Hydroptilidae; *Oxyethira serrata, pallida, michiganensis.*
   d. **Body bright yellow, orange brown and shades in between, wings gray to brown, can be solid or spotted, legs yellow to black, 2.5-4mm,** spring to fall **(Vari-Colored Microcaddis)**. Three important species W, *H. acoma, rono, argosa*, three species E M W, *H. ajax, hamata, consimilis,* three species E M, *H. jackmanni, albicornis, waubesiana.* Color and size can vary even in the same species.
   e. **Color other than a. to c.** Hydroptilidae; *Hydroptila* species.

11. a. **Body yellow with a purplish tinge, wings brown, legs yellow, 5-6mm,** July to first week in August **(Dinky Purple-Breasted Sedge)** Psychomyiidae; *Psychomyia flavida.* (See Note C for diagnostic verification).**
   b. **Body amber, wings light brown with heavy speckling of dark brown appearing black, 5-7mm,** emergence mid-May **(Speckled Peter)** Helicopsychidae; *Helicopsyche borealis.* (See Note B for diagnostic verification).**
   c. **Body green, wings black, legs dark gray, 6-7.5mm, mid-June to mid-July (Little Western Weedy Water Sedge)** Brachycentridae; *Micrasema bactro.* (See Note E for diagnostic verification).**
   d. **Body grayish-black, wings grayish-black with a few light speckles, legs gray, 5-7mm,** mid-May to late June **(Little Black Short-Horned Sedge)** Glossosomatidae; *Glossosoma montana.* (See Note D for diagnostic verification).**
   e. **Body dark gray with bright green lateral line, wings very dark gray, legs gray, 6-7mm (male),** late August to September on Bighorn River, **(Little Grannom)** Brachycentridae; *Amiocentrus aspilus.* **Note:** Females can be as large as 9mm. (See Note E for diagnostic verification).**

12. a. **Body, males blue-green, females yellow, wings light gray, legs tan, 10-12mm,** first of June to late July **(Gray Wing Long-Horned Sedge)** Leptoceridae; *Oecetis disjuncta.*
   b. **Body yellow or yellow-olive, wings light brown with dark brown spots, legs ginger, 10-12mm,** mid-June to mid-August, E M W **(Tan Spotted Wing Long-Horned Sedge)** Leptoceridae; *Oecetis avara.*
   c. **Body dark green to dull amber, wings black, antennae light gray with black rings and very long, 8-9mm,** mid-July to late August, **(Black Dancer)** Leptoceridae; *Mystacides alafimbriata.*

13. a. **Body olive, wings grayish-brown usually with a little tan or cream mottling, legs tannish-brown, 7-9mm, wing type D,** Mid-June to late August, **(Little Sister Sedge)** Hydropsychidae; *Cheumatopsyche lassa, pettiti.* (See Note G for diagnostic verification).**
   b. **Body very dark grayish-brown, almost black, with a green lateral line, wings gray with black veins, legs paler gray, male 7-8mm, female 9-10mm, mid-April to mid-June with explosive emergence (Little Black Caddis)** Brachycentridae; *Brachycentrus occidentalis.* (See Note F for diagnostic verification).**

c. **Body olive, wings plain brown, (males have a dark gray recurve on leading edge of wings which is an easy identifying characteristic, 8-10mm,** mid-June to late August W **(Little Plain Brown Sedge)** Lepidostomatidae; *Lepidostoma pluviale.* (See Note L for diagnostic verification).**

14. a. **Body light to medium brown, wing grayish-brown with a mottled pattern of light and dark areas, 8-12mm, wing type D,** mid-May to last of August **(Spotted Sedge)** Hydropsychidae; *Hydropsyche cockerelli, occidentalis, oslari, placoda.* (The species' are in order of seasonal emergence). (See Note J for diagnostic verification).**

b. **Body grayish-brown, wings grayish-brown with pale flecks, especially around apex, late July to end of August, male 7-10mm, female 11-13mm (Grannom)** Brachycentridae; *Brachycentrus americanus.* (See Note F for diagnostic verification).**

15. a. **Body olive green, wing gray and brown mottled, legs ginger, 12-16mm, July one to last of October, first species July one to August 30, second species September 5 to October 25, (Green Sedge)** Rhyacophilidae; *Rhyacophila bifida, coloradensis.* (See Note H for diagnostic verification).**

16. a. **Body green to greenish-brown, wing brownish-gray with lighter spotting, legs brown, 17-20mm, wing type D,** late June to second week in July **(Great Gray Spotted Sedge)** Hydropsychidae; *Arctopsyche grandis.* (See Note J for diagnostic verification).**

b. **Body olive, wing golden ginger with black and silver stripes, legs yellow, 17-20mm,** July 15 to August 5 **(Silver Striped Sedge)** Limnephilidae; *Hesperophylax designatus.* (See Note K for diagnostic verification).**

c. **Body olive, wing golden ginger with black and silver stripes, legs yellow, 27-34mm, (Silver Striped Sedge)** Limnephilidae; *Hesperophylax incisis.* (See Note K for diagnostic verification).**

d. **Body reddish-orange, wing mottled gray and brown, legs light brown, 20-30mm,** September to first weeks of October **(Giant Orange Sedge)** Limnephilidae; *Dicosmoecus atripes, gilvipes, jucundus.*

e. **Body cinnamon brown, females with olive tinge, legs and antennae cinnamon brown, wings tan with three brown marks in the middle of wing and a dark line on top of wing and a translucent line below the brown marks,** emergence September and October on Bighorn River, not known elsewhere in Montana **(Autumn Sedge)** Limnephilidae; *Limnephilus thorus.* (See Note K for diagnostic verification).**

Diagnostic Verification for Fishermen's Keys to Caddisflies

FIGURE 1

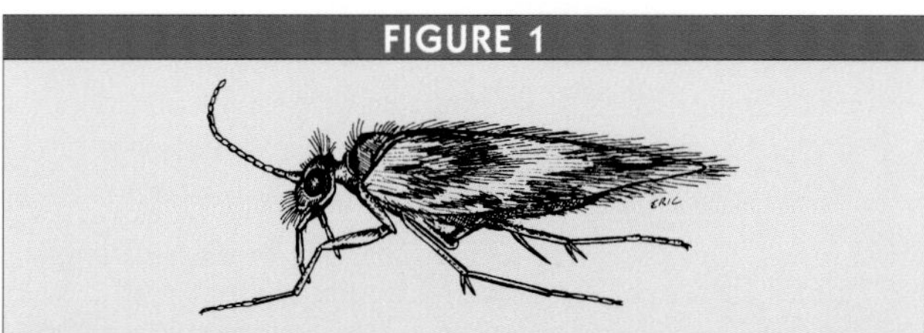

Figure 1: Small, very hairy forms. (Family: Hydroptilidae)

FIGURE 2

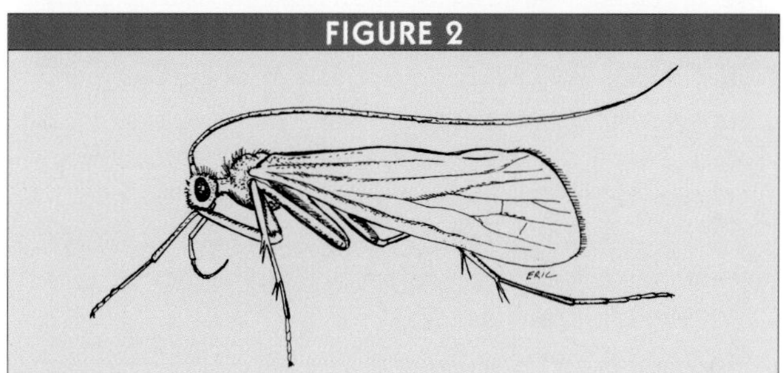

Figure 2: Small forms, not hairy. (Family: Glossosomatidae; Genus: *Protoptila*)

FIGURE 3

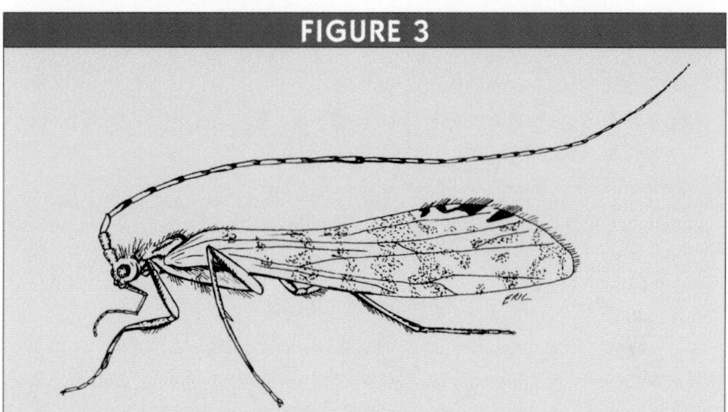

Figure 3: Antennae more than twice the length of body. (Family: Leptoceridae)

FIGURE 4

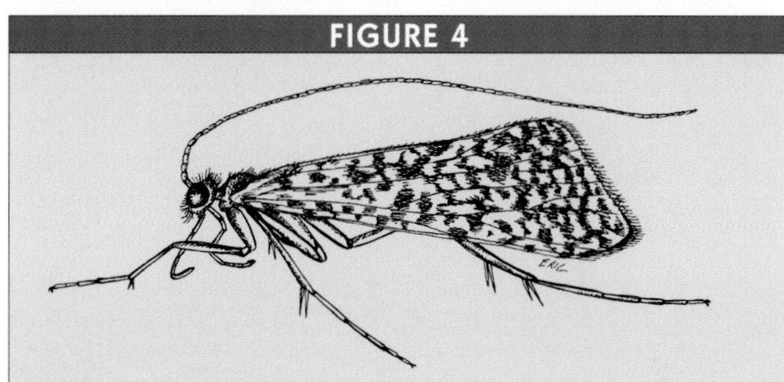

Figure 4: Antennae less than twice the length of body. (All the rest of the families)

Note A: Diagnostic verification; See Key to the Families under Philopotamidae

Note B: Diagnostic verification; See Key to the Families under Helicopsychidae

Note C: Diagnostic verification; See Key to the Families under Psychomyiidae

Note D: Diagnostic verification; See Key to the Families under Glossosomatidae

Note E: Diagnostic verification; See Key to the Families under Brachycentridae and Key to the Genera of Brachycentridae under *Micrasema*

Note F: Diagnostic verification; See Key to the Families under Brachycentridae and Key to the Genera of Brachycentridae under *Brachycentrus*

Note G: Diagnostic verification; See Key to the Families under Hydropsychidae and Key to the Genera of Hydropsychidae under *Cheumatopsyche*

Note H: Diagnostic verification; See Key to the Families under Rhyacophilidae

Note I: Diagnostic verification; See Key to the Families under Polycentropodidae

Note J: Diagnostic verification; See Key to the Families under Hydropsychidae and Key to the Genera of Hydropsychidae under *Ceratopsyche* and *Hydropsyche*

Note K: Diagnostic verification; See Key to the Families under Limnephilidae

Note L: Diagnostic verification; See Key to the Families under Leptostomatidae

Note M: Diagnostic verification; See Key to the Families under Hydropsychidae under *Potamyia*

Note N: Diagnostic verification; See Key to the Families under Molannidae

Note O: Diagnostic verification; See Key to the Families under Phryganeidae

Note P: Diagnostic verification; See Key to the Families under Odontoceridae

Wing Types

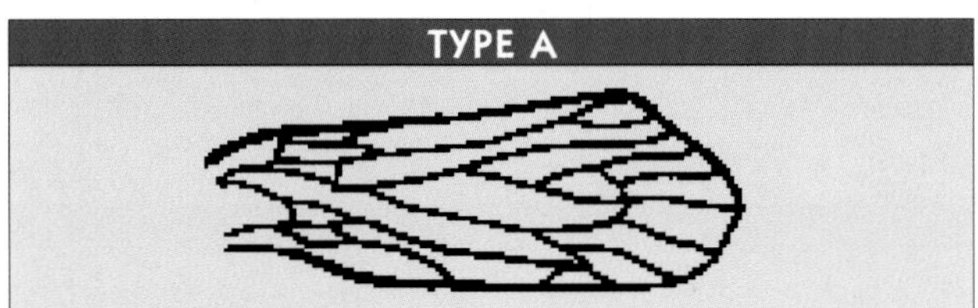

Type A: Family Brachycentridae, Limnephilidae, Lepidostomatidae.

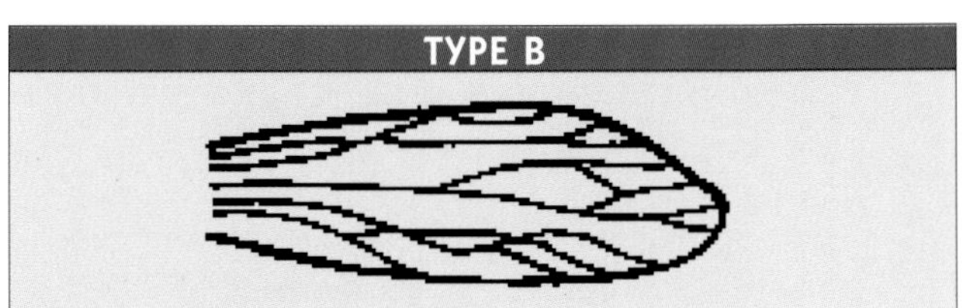

Type B: Family Phryganeidae.

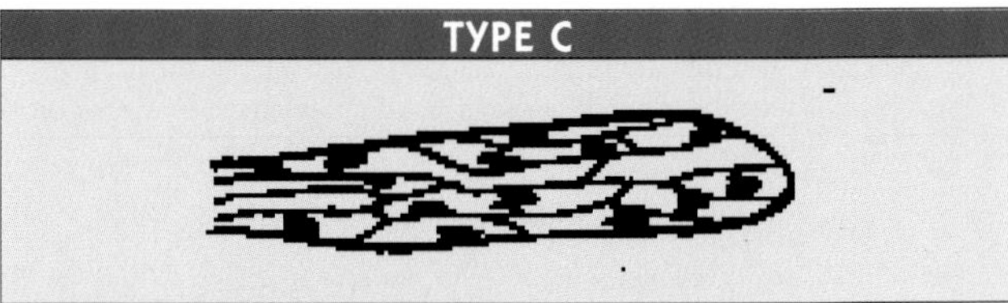

Type C: Family Leptoceridae.

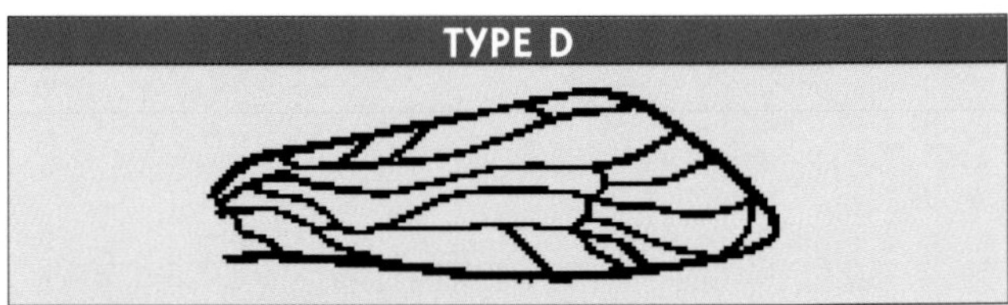

Type D: Family Hydropsychidae.

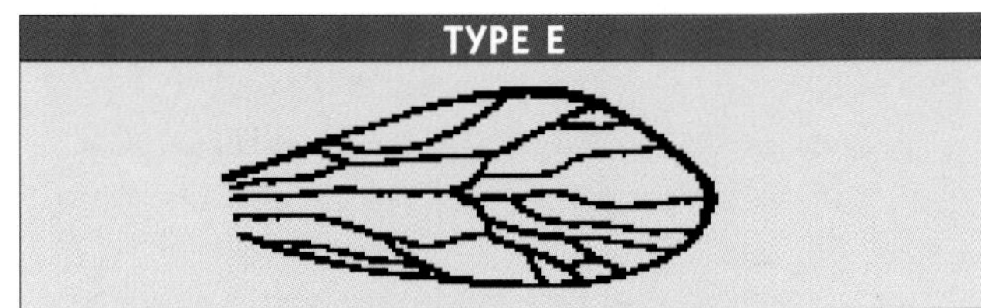

Type E: Family Odontoceridae, Goeridae, Helicopsychidae.

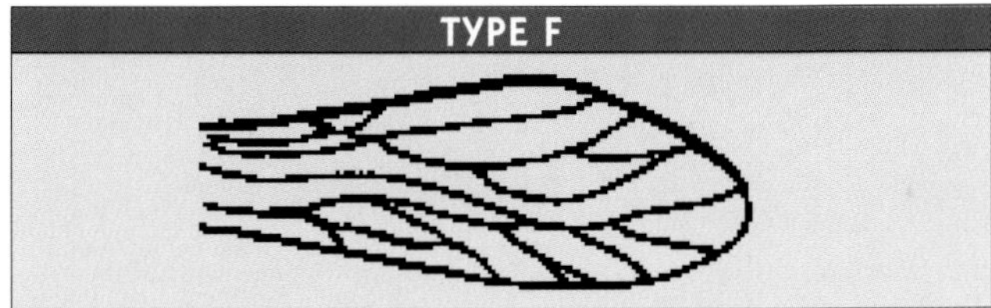

Type F: Family Rhyacophilidae, Philopotamidae, Polycentropodae.

Seasonal Distribution of Eastern Caddisflies
= Indicates total emergence period.
= Indicates heaviest emergence and selective feeding by trout. This hatch chart for the longitude of northeastern Pennsylvania. Hatch times will be later to the north and earlier to the south.
Apr.
May
June
July
Aug.
Sept.
Oct.
Nov.
Summer Flier
Limnephilus submonilifer
Early Smoky Wing Sedge
Apatania incerta
Little Summer Olive, a k a Little Sister Sedge
Cheumatopsyche pettiti, harwoodi
Little Black Caddis, a k a Grannom
Brachycentrus species'
B. lateralis
B. numerosus
B. americanus
B. solomoni
B. appalachia
Tiny Black Caddis
Chimarra aterrima
Little Black Short-Horned Sedge
Glossosoma nigrior
Little Grannom
Micrasema rusticum
Cinnamon Sedge
Ceratopsyche bronta
True Microcaddis
Hydroptilidae sp.
Pseudo Microcaddis
Glossosomatidae sp.
Green Sedge
Rhyacophila fuscula
Little Gray Sedge
Goera calcarata
Chocolate and Cream Sedge
Platycentropus radiatus
Speckled Peter
Helicopsyche borealis
Gray Checkered Sedge
Molanna unipola, cinera
Dinky Purple-Breasted Sedge
Psychomyia flavida
Dark Woodland Sedge
Lype diversa
White Miller
Nectopsyche albida, exquisita, diarina
Black Dancer and Golden Wing Dancer
Mystacides interjecta, sepulchralis
Brown Scaly Wing Sedge
Ceraclea transversa, arieles
Little Plain Brown Sedge
Lepidostoma togatum, vernalis
Black and Tan-Patterned Wing Sedge, a k a Zebra Sedge
Micronema zebratum
Silver Striped Sedge
Hesperophylax designatus
Tan Long-Horned Sedge
Oecetis avara, inconspicua
Giant Cream-Patterned Wing Sedge
Hydratophylax argus
Brown Checkered Summer Sedge
Polycentropus cinereus
Dinky Light Summer Sedge
Nyctiophylax moestus
Dark Blue Sedge
Psilotreta labia
Great Brown Autumn Sedge
Pycnopsyche lepida, guttifer
Dot Wing Sedge
Frenesia missa

Seasonal Distribution of Midwestern Caddisflies

■ = Indicates total emergence period.

■ = Indicates heaviest emergence and selective feeding by trout. This hatch chart for the longitude of the middle of the lower peninsula of Michigan. Hatch times will be earlier the farther south you go. The Mad River in Ohio is about three weeks ahead of Michigan. The South Holsten in north-eastern Tennessee is about six weeks ahead of Michigan.

Apr. | May | June | July | Aug. | Sept. | Oct. | Nov.

Summer Flier
Limnephilus sericus, submolifer

Little Summer Olive, a k a Little Sister Sedge
Cheumatopsyche species

Little Black Caddis, a k a Grannom
Brachycentrus species'
B. lateralis
B. numerosus
B. americanus

Tiny Black Caddis
Chimarra ferra, aterrima

Little Black Short-Horned Sedge
Glossosoma nigrior

Little Grannom
Micrasema rusticum

Cinnamon Sedge
Ceratopsyche species' *bifila, recurvata, phalerata, sparna, slossonae, bronta*

True Microcaddis
Hydroptilidae sp.

***Pseudo* Microcaddis**
Glossosomatidae sp.

Green Sedge
Rhyacophila manistee, melita

Little Gray Sedge
Goera stylata

Chocolate and Cream Sedge
Platycentropus radiatus

Speckled Peter
Helicopsyche borealis

Gray Checkered Sedge
Molanna unipola

Little Red Twilight Sedge
Neureclipsis crepuscularis

Giant Rusty Sedge
Ptilostomis ocellifera, semifaciata

Apr. | May | June | July | Aug. | Sept. | Oct. | Nov.

Dark Woodland Sedge
Lype diversa

White Miller
Nectopsyche albida

Black Dancer and Golden Wing Dancer
Mystacides interjecta, sepulchralis

Brown Scaly Wing Sedge
Ceraclea transversa, arieles

Little Plain Brown Sedge
Lepidostoma
1st *bryanti*
2nd *costalis*
3rd *togatum*

Black and Tan-Patterned Wing Sedge, a k a Zebra Sedge
Macronema zebratum

Silver Striped Sedge
Hesperophylax designatus

Tan Long-Horned Sedge
Oecetis avara, inconspicua

Giant Cream-Patterned Wing Sedge
Hydratophylax argus

Yellow Sedge
Potamyia flava

Brown Checkered Summer Sedge
Polycentropus cinereus

Dinky Light Summer Sedge
Nyctiophylax moestus

Minute Gray Wing Cinnamon Sedge
Glossosomatidae; *Protoptila immaculata*

Great Brown Autumn Sedge
Pycnopsyche lepida, guttifer

Small Dot Wing Sedge
Neophylax (now *Uenoidae) fuscous*

Dot Wing Sedge
Frenesia missa

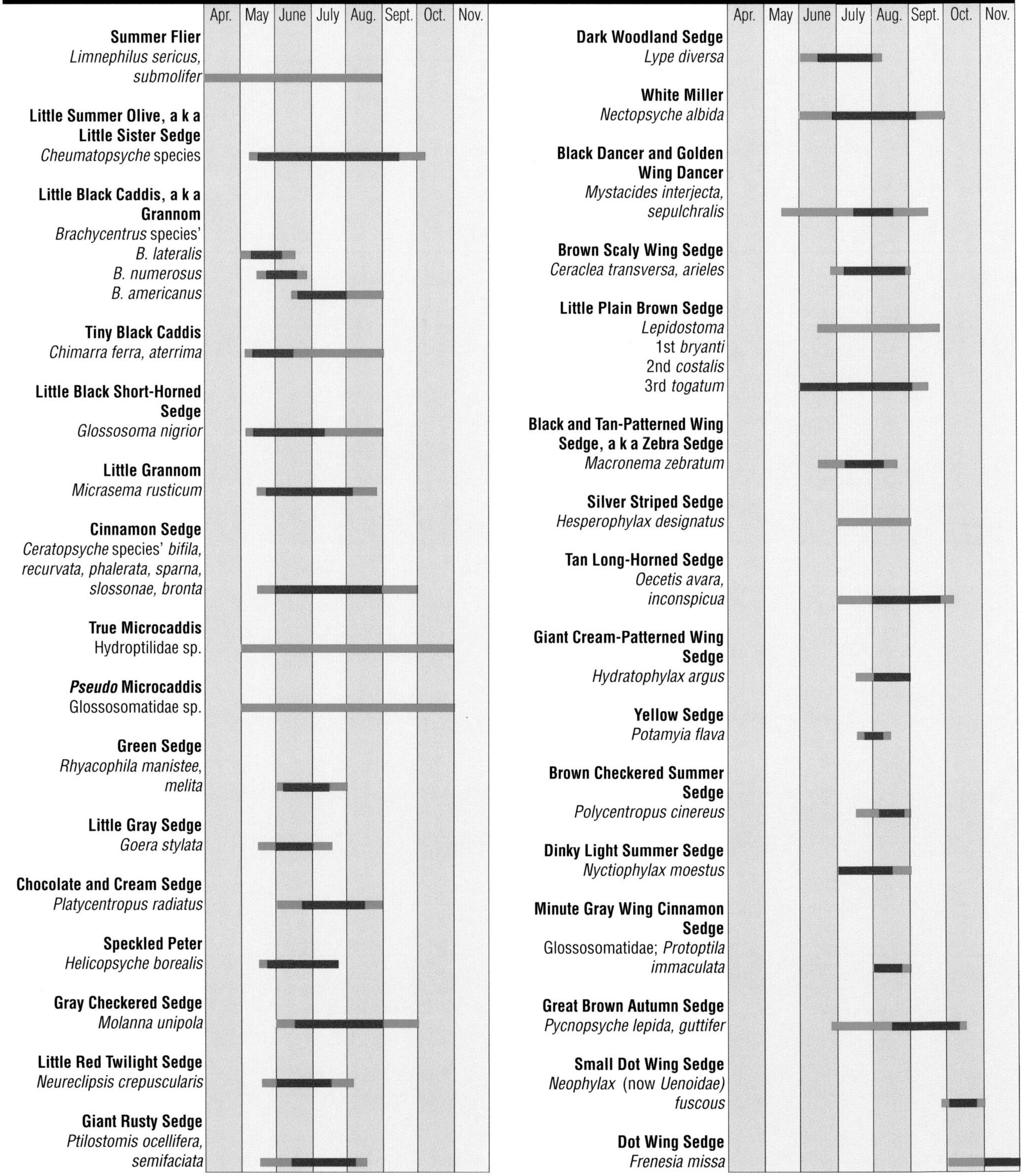

Seasonal Distribution of Western Caddisflies

■ = Indicates total emergence period.

■ = Indicates heaviest emergence and selective feeding by trout. This hatch chart for southern Montana, Idaho, northern Wyoming. Hatch times can vary quite a bit depending on altitude, type of stream (tailwater, spring creek, freestone) and longitude.

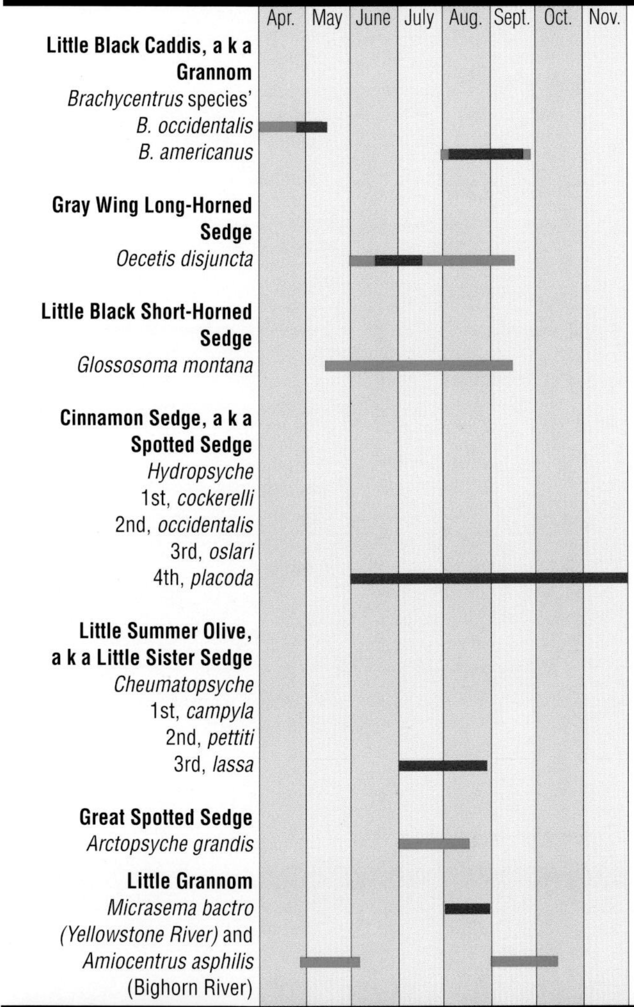

Apr.
May
June
July
Aug.
Sept.
Oct.
Nov.
Little Black Caddis, a k a Grannom
Brachycentrus species'
B. occidentalis
B. americanus
Gray Wing Long-Horned Sedge
Oecetis disjuncta
Little Black Short-Horned Sedge
Glossosoma montana
Cinnamon Sedge, a k a Spotted Sedge
Hydropsyche
1st, cockerelli
2nd, occidentalis
3rd, oslari
4th, placoda
Little Summer Olive, a k a Little Sister Sedge
Cheumatopsyche
1st, campyla
2nd, pettiti
3rd, lassa
Great Spotted Sedge
Arctopsyche grandis
Little Grannom
Micrasema bactro
(Yellowstone River) and
Amiocentrus asphilis
(Bighorn River)

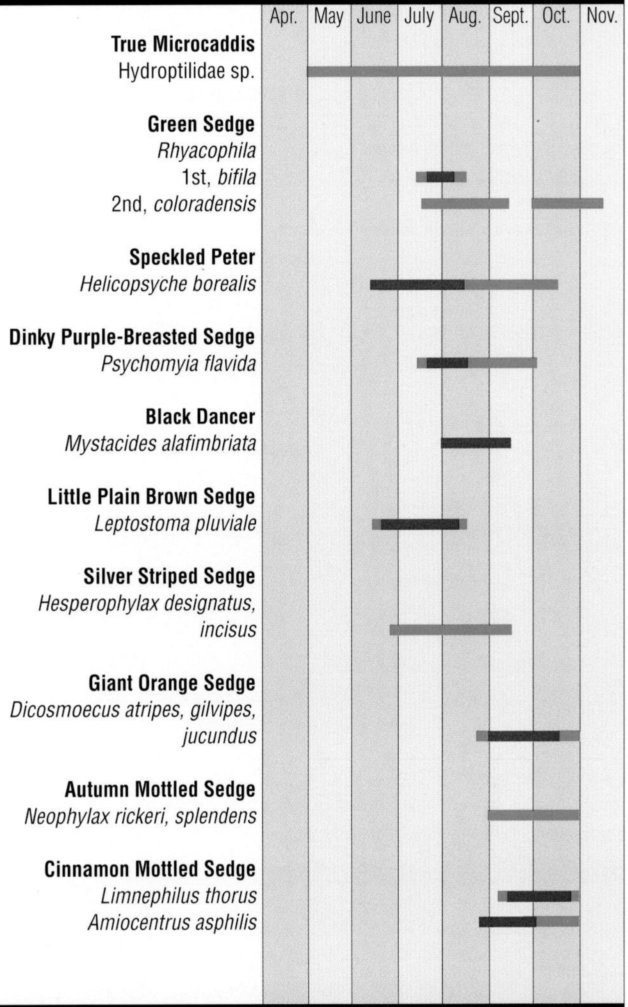

Apr.
May
June
July
Aug.
Sept.
Oct.
Nov.
True Microcaddis
Hydroptilidae sp.
Green Sedge
Rhyacophila
1st, bifila
2nd, coloradensis
Speckled Peter
Helicopsyche borealis
Dinky Purple-Breasted Sedge
Psychomyia flavida
Black Dancer
Mystacides alafimbriata
Little Plain Brown Sedge
Leptostoma pluviale
Silver Striped Sedge
Hesperophylax designatus, incisus
Giant Orange Sedge
Dicosmoecus atripes, gilvipes, jucundus
Autumn Mottled Sedge
Neophylax rickeri, splendens
Cinnamon Mottled Sedge
Limnephilus thorus
Amiocentrus asphilis

Seasonal Distribution of Appalachian South Caddisflies

■ = Indicates total emergence period.

■ = Indicates heaviest emergence and selective feeding by trout. This hatch chart for the longitude of eastern Tennessee. Hatch times will be later to the north and earlier to the south, and vary at different elevations.

Apr.
May
June
July
Aug.
Sept.
Oct.
Nov.
Little Summer Olive, a k a Little Sister Sedge
Cheumatopsyche
miniscula
campyla
pettiti

Apr.
May
June
July
Aug.
Sept.
Oct.
Nov.
Little Black Caddis, aka Grannom
Brachycentrus species
B. numerosus
B. spinae
B. etowahensis
B. lateralis
B. appalachia

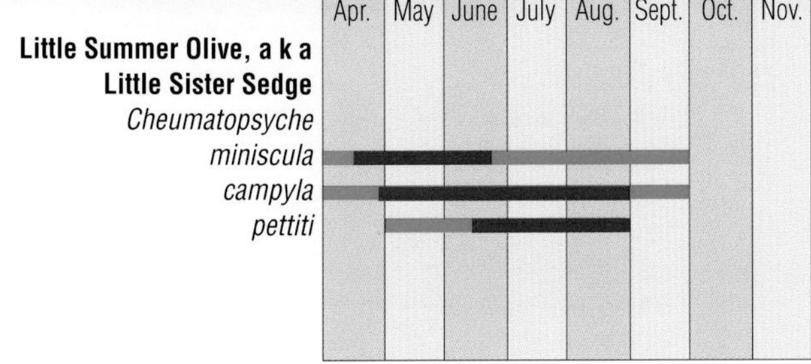

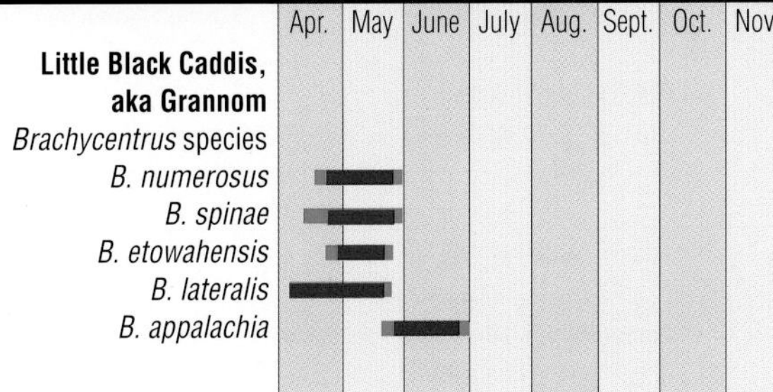

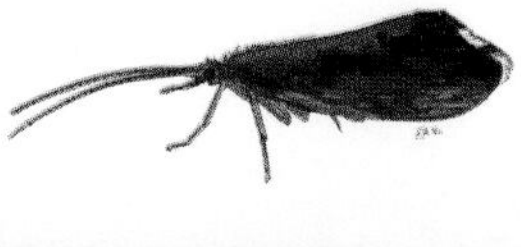

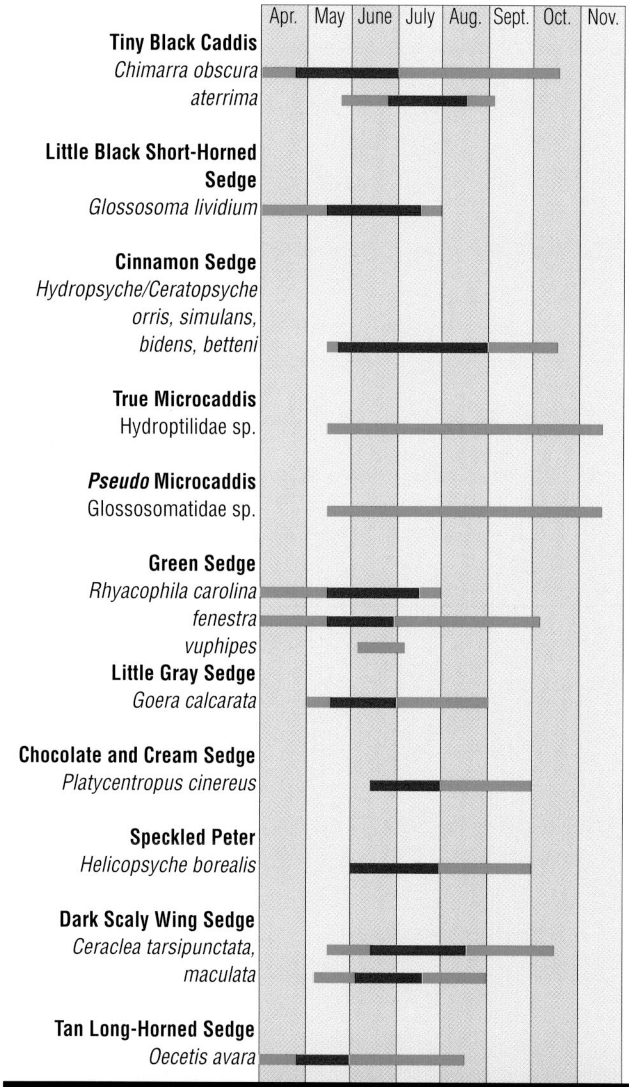

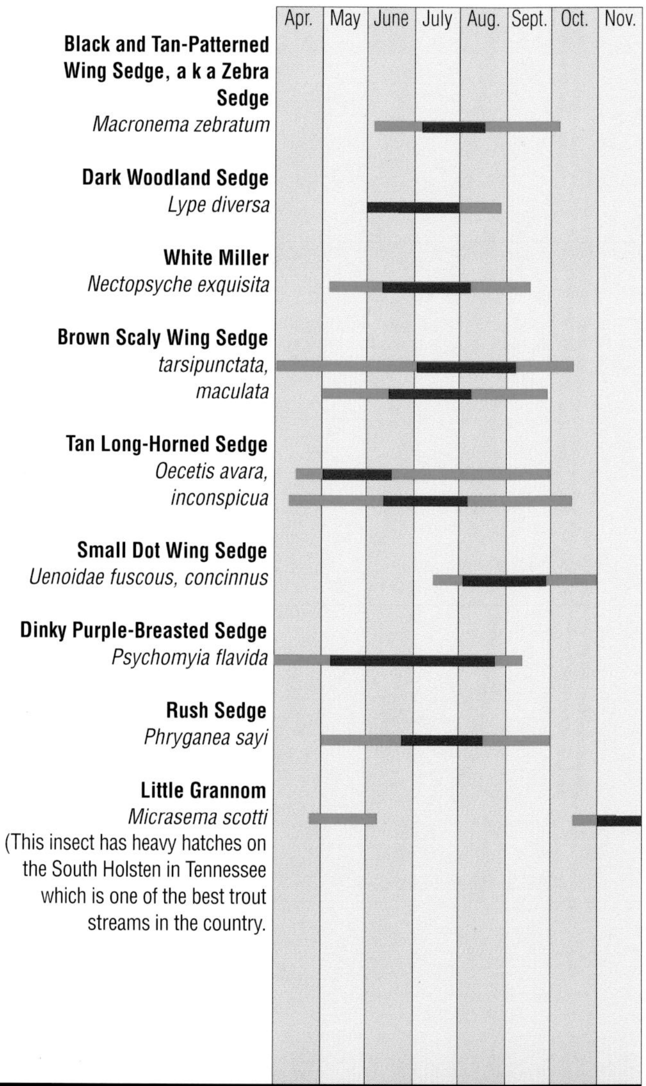

Apr. | May | June | July | Aug. | Sept. | Oct. | Nov.

Tiny Black Caddis
Chimarra obscura
aterrima

Little Black Short-Horned Sedge
Glossosoma lividium

Cinnamon Sedge
Hydropsyche/Ceratopsyche orris, simulans, bidens, betteni

True Microcaddis
Hydroptilidae sp.

***Pseudo* Microcaddis**
Glossosomatidae sp.

Green Sedge
Rhyacophila carolina
fenestra
vuphipes

Little Gray Sedge
Goera calcarata

Chocolate and Cream Sedge
Platycentropus cinereus

Speckled Peter
Helicopsyche borealis

Dark Scaly Wing Sedge
Ceraclea tarsipunctata,
maculata

Tan Long-Horned Sedge
Oecetis avara

Apr. | May | June | July | Aug. | Sept. | Oct. | Nov.

Black and Tan-Patterned Wing Sedge, a k a Zebra Sedge
Macronema zebratum

Dark Woodland Sedge
Lype diversa

White Miller
Nectopsyche exquisita

Brown Scaly Wing Sedge
tarsipunctata,
maculata

Tan Long-Horned Sedge
Oecetis avara,
inconspicua

Small Dot Wing Sedge
Uenoidae fuscous, concinnus

Dinky Purple-Breasted Sedge
Psychomyia flavida

Rush Sedge
Phryganea sayi

Little Grannom
Micrasema scotti
(This insect has heavy hatches on the South Holsten in Tennessee which is one of the best trout streams in the country.

Seasonal Distribution of Pacific Northwest Caddisflies

■ = Indicates total emergence period.

■ = Indicates heaviest emergence and selective feeding by trout. This hatch chart for Oregon. Hatch times can vary quite a bit depending on altitude, type of stream (tailwater, spring creek, freestone) and longitude.

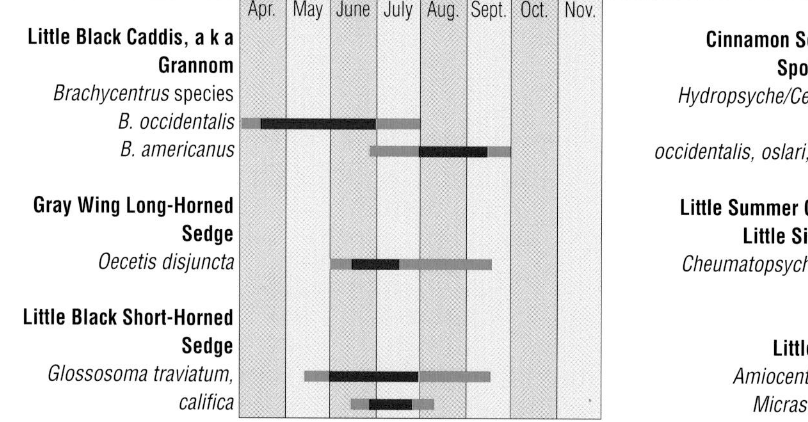

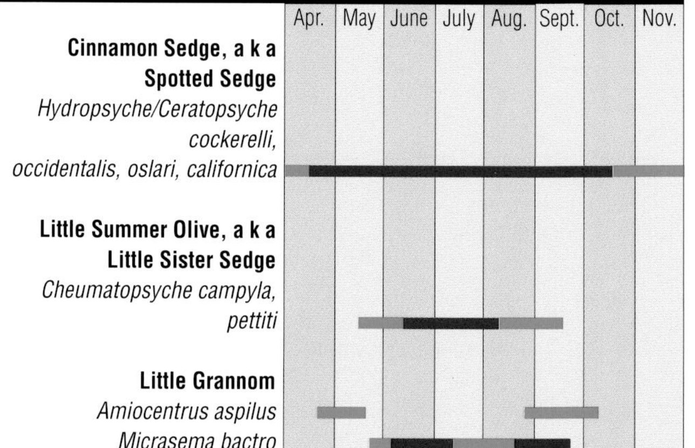

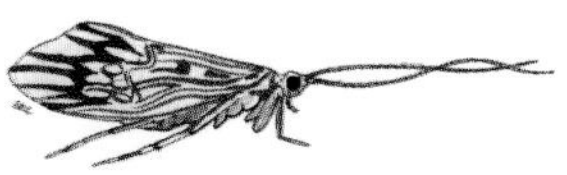

Apr. May June July Aug. Sept. Oct. Nov.

True Microcaddis
Hydroptilidae sp.

Green Sedge
Rhyacophila grandis,
bifila,
vaccum

Speckled Peter
Helicopsyche borealis

Black Dancer
Mystacides alafimbriata

Little Plain Brown Sedge
Leptostoma rayneri
Leptostoma unicolor

Apr. May June July Aug. Sept. Oct. Nov.

Silver Striped Sedge
Hesperophylax incisus

Giant Orange Sedge
Dicosmoecus atripes,
gilvipes

Autumn Mottled Sedge
Neophylax rickeri,
splendens

Cinnamon Mottled Sedge
Limnephilus thorus

Seasonal Distribution of *Hydropsyche* and *Ceratopsyche* (Trichoptera)

■ = Indicates total emergence period.

■ = Indicates heaviest emergence and selective feeding by trout.

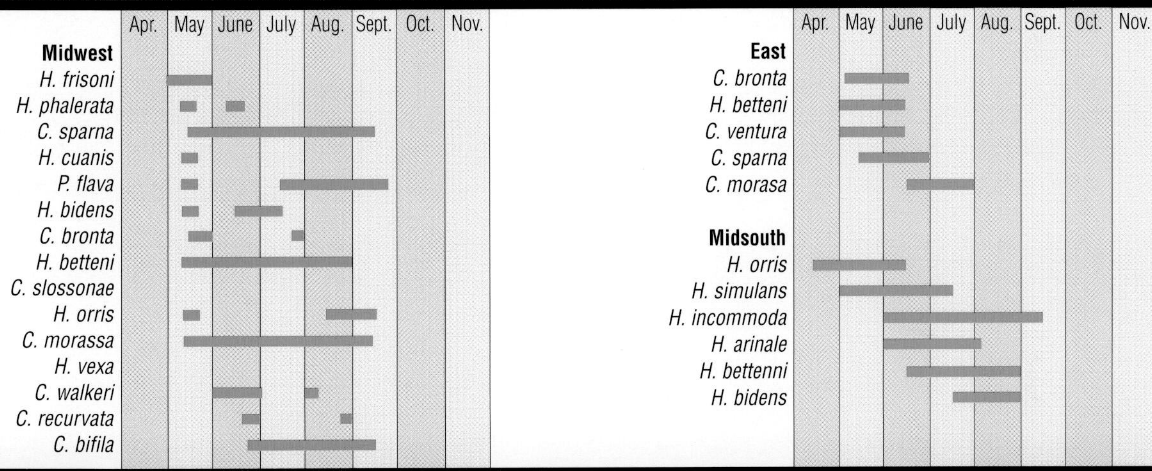

Seasonal Distribution of *Cheumatopsyche* (Trichoptera)

■ = Indicates total emergence period.

■ = Indicates heaviest emergence and selective feeding by trout.

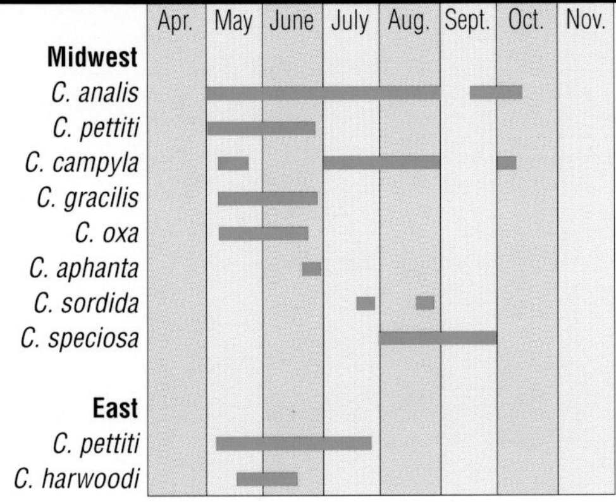

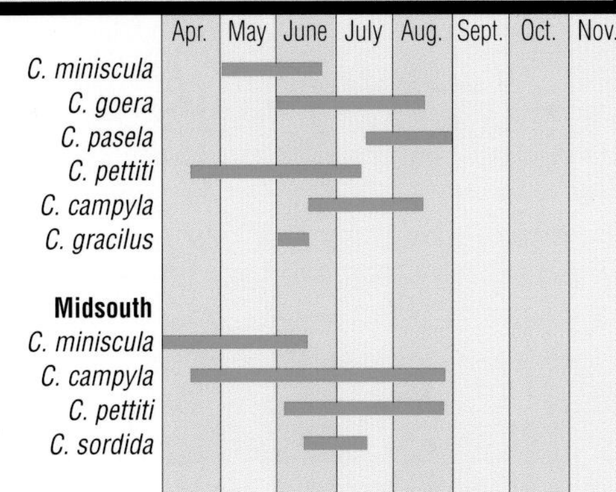

Chapter V

DESCRIPTIONS OF THE FAMILIES, GENERA AND SPECIES

Family Hydropsychidae

Genera

Ceratopsyche (Cinnamon Sedge, a k a Spotted Sedge)
Hydropsyche (Window Winged Sedge)
Cheumatopsyche (Little Olive Sedge)
Arctopsyche (Great Gray Spotted Wing Sedge)
Macronema (Zebra Wing Caddis, a k a Black and Tan-Patterned Wing Sedge)
Potamyia (Yellow Sedge)

Ceratopsyche bifila seen from below.

The Family Hydropsychidae is far and away the most important group of caddis to fishermen over the entire year. They start early in the spring, last to almost the end of the season and hatch in a coordinated fashion with good numbers. The Genera *Ceratopsyche*, (Spotted Sedge or Cinnamon Sedge) and *Hydropsyche* (Window Wing Sedge) are the most important group of caddisflies for trout fishermen with about 70 species in the United States which fortunately all look pretty much alike. The old *bifila* group of *Hydropsyche*, (Ross, 44) has been renamed genus *Ceratopsyche*. This group was called *Symphitopsyche* by some workers for awhile but this term is no longer valid for American caddisflies.

The *bifila* group, now *Ceratopsyche,* consists of *C. bifila, cheilonie, recurvata, walkeri, bronta, morosa, riola,*

Glossosoma nigrior pupa.

alhedra, slossonae, macleodi, sparna, ventura, piatrix and *etnieri*. This is the group called the Spotted Sedge. The *depravata* group stays in *Hydropsyche* and the insects are also called Spotted Sedge. It consists of *H. betteni, depravata, potomacensis, elissoma, decalda* and *carolina*. The *cuanis* group consists of one species, *H. cuanis* and is similar in appearance to the first two groups. The *scalaris* group stays in *Hydropsyche*. This is the group we call the Window Wing Sedge because they have a pattern in the wing which when observed from the top looks like a little tan window in the middle of the vertex of the folded wings. The group consists of *H. oris, bidens, aerata, phalerata, dicantha, demora, valanis, arinale, scalaris, simulans, incomoda, frisoni, mississippiensis, hoffmani, leonardi, hageni* and *patera*. This group looks different from the other groups, but the difference is in the top of the wing and the fish cannot see it unless the insect is swimming up

HYDROPSYCHE SIMULANS

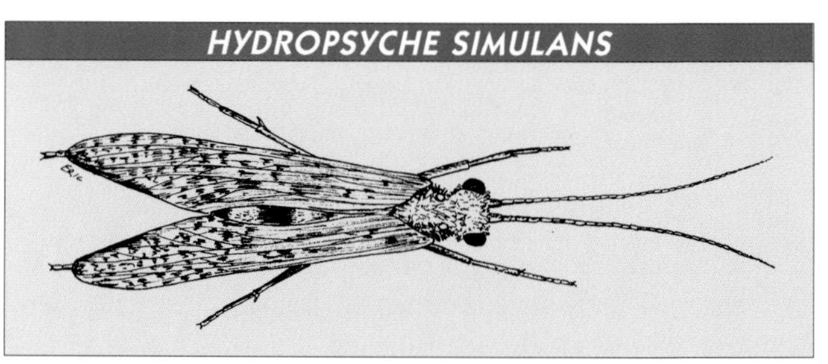

from the bottom after egg laying so it is difficult to rationalize the need to imitate the window pattern in an artificial, except for a wet fly.

Cheumatopsyche analis pupa from a trout's stomach.

The genus *Cheumatopsyche* is only slightly less important than *Ceratopsyche* and *Hydropsyche* for fishermen. It also has many species which are very similar and are widespread from the East to the West. This is the Little Green Sedge or Little Sister Sedge.

Genus *Macronema* has only one significant species, *zebratum*, which is important on warmer Eastern and Midwestern trout streams. It is very large and a daytime emerger. It is called the zebra caddis because of its black and yellow striped wings.

Arctopsyche grandus, a Western species, is mostly nocturnal but is very large in size so an adult imitation is useful as a daytime searching pattern. The larvae are large and active and imitations fished on the bottom catch a lot of fish. They are the Great Gray Spotted Sedges.

Potamyia has one species, *flava*, which is the same size as *Hydropsyche* but is very light brownish-yellow and is a common large-stream species found in the Midwestern and Southern states. These are the Yellow Sedges.

The pupae of Hydropsychidae emerge by swimming to the surface. The downstream drift of the pupae before it swims to the surface is longer than most caddis species and

Ceratopsyche bifila emerger adult stuck in shuck from trout's stomach.

trout feed on the pupae long before surface activity is apparent. The time the pupa takes struggling out of its shuck is also much longer than most other families. Because of this, trout feed on the pupae, emergers and

CERATOPSYCHE PUPA

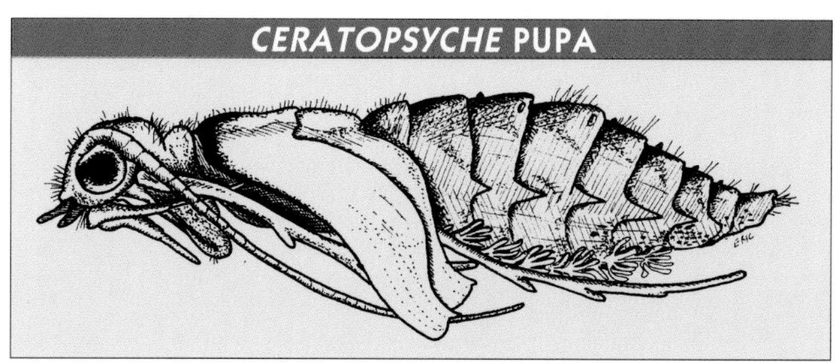

adults and will take imitations of each, but feed on the pupae first. Most emergence activity is in the evening but can occur in the morning or even at midday. In the Midwest, *Cheumatopsyche analis* is an evening emerger in August but switches to mornings in September.

Egg laying with most Hydropsychidae has morning and evening peaks but occurs sporadically all day. It is accomplished by females crawling under the water and sprawling or bouncing on the surface. A wet fly works well at these times. A spent quad wing imitation is very useful in the late evening after ovipositing.

Ceratopsyche bifila.

Ceratopsyche larva (tan and gray). *Cheumatopsyche* larva (green).

Hook Sizes:

Ceratopsyche and *Hydropsyche*: 16-18
Cheumatopsyche: 18-22
Arctopysche: 8-10
Macronema: 14
Potamyia: 16-18

Larval Type: Common netspinner.

Most Important Species of *Hydropsyche* and *Ceratopsyche*

1. *C. cockerelli* (Cinnamon Sedge, a k a Spotted Sedge and Window Wing Sedge)....W

2. *H. occidentalis* .... W
3. *H. oslari* .... W
4. *H. placoda* .... W
5. *C. bifila* .... W
6. *H. recurvata* .... M
7. *H. phalerata* .... M
8. *C. sparna* .... E M
9. *C. slossonae* .... E M W
10. *C. bronta* .... E M W

Length: 8-12mm.
Color: Body cinnamon to very light brown, almost yellow, with grayish-brown wings which have a speckling of light tan spots (*bifila* group), the legs are cinnamon and the antennae are tan with darker rings. The *scalaris* group have a light tan pattern on the top of the wings. This pattern looks like a little window in the wing when seen from the top. This group includes *H. phalerata* and *H. simulans*, which are the most common species in the group. A few species have olive bodies at emergence which turn brown later. These can be differentiated from *Cheumatopsyche* by their larger size and by using the key to the genera of Hydropsychidae in the back of this book. Emergence is from May to September.

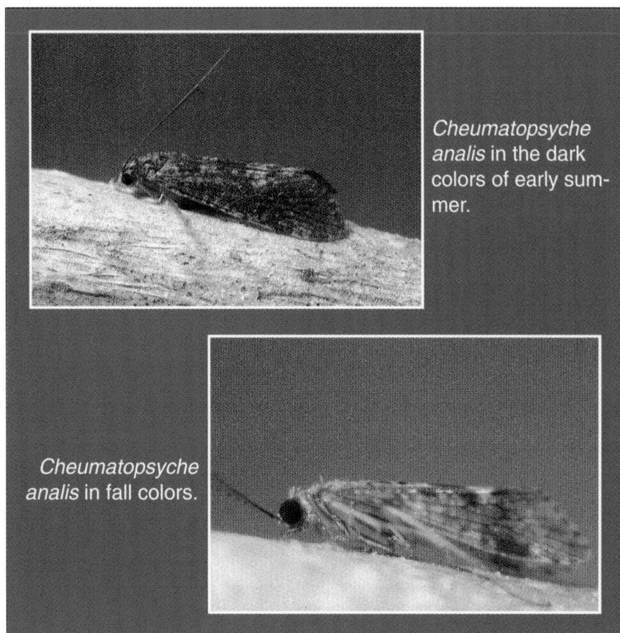
Cheumatopsyche analis in the dark colors of early summer.

Cheumatopsyche analis in fall colors.

Most Important Species of *Cheumatopsyche*

1. *C. pettiti=analis* (Little Green Sedge, a k a Little Sister Sedge) .... E M W
2. *C. lassa* .... E M W
3. *C. campyla* .... E M W
4. *C. spesiosa* .... M
5. *C. harwoodi* .... E
6. *C. gracilis* .... E M W
7. *C. oxa* .... E M W S

Cheumatopsyche larva.

Length: 7-9mm, a few species are a little larger, to 12mm.
Color: Body green, which becomes lighter as the season progresses. Wings are dark grayish-brown with a few lighter markings early in the emergence and becoming a lighter gray with more apparent tannish spots later in the emergence. Some species have more lighter spots than others, *C. spesiosa* and *C. analis* have the most. The legs are amber and the antennae are amber with darker bands.
Emergence: June to late September.

Species *Arctopsyche*

1. *A. grandus* .... W

Length: 17-20mm.
Color: Body is bright olive to brownish-olive depending on the river. Wings are grayish-brown with lighter brown speckles. The antennae are brown with darker rings and the legs are brown.
Emergence: Late June to early July at night.

Macronema zebratum showing body color.

Species *Macronema*

1. *M. zebratum* .... E M

Length: 15-18mm.
Color: Body is black with lighter rings. Wings are black with distinctive tannish-yellow pattern. The legs are ginger and the antennae are very long (41mm) and black.
Emergence: Early to late August on Eastern and Midwestern tailwater rivers and warmer trout streams. This is a very large insect which emerges in late

afternoon and evening, often in huge numbers, and rates super hatch status on warmer rivers, such as the Housatonic in Connecticut, Androscoggin in New Hampshire and Maine, Muskegon in Michigan, as well as other streams in Pennsylvania and Massachusetts.

Species *Potamyia*

1. *P. flava* .... M W S

Length: 10-11mm.
Color: Uniformly light brownish-yellow with a slight pinkish tinge. Males have very long, slender antennae and lack spurs on the front tibia. Females have normal spurs and shorter antennae.
Emergence: Early May to early fall mostly from large rivers. This insect can hatch in huge numbers on rivers where it is found.

Family Brachycentridae

Genera

Brachycentrus (Little Black Caddis, a k a Grannom)
Ameocentrus Micrasema (Little Weedy Water Sedge, a k a Tiny Grannom)

The species of these genera generally emerge in spring with explosive numbers, but the hatches last only two or three weeks. This makes them the most important group for fly fishermen at this time. The hatches begin just after opening day in many areas and when the weather is becoming very pleasant. The insects fly in the early afternoon and their egg laying takes place in late afternoon to evening, although it can coincide with the emergence. The pupae emerge in midstream and drift for 10 to 20 feet while struggling out of the pupal shuck. Once out of it, two flaps of their wings and they are off the water quickly. Ovipositing is by sprawling on the water and by crawling under water. The males are smaller than the females by one hook size. Most fly fishermen are on the water after the long winter and since these caddisflies produce heavy feeding by trout most anglers are very familiar with these insects. The one species in this group that is an exception to these early and explosive emergences is *B. americanus,* which hatches a little later in the year with fewer numbers, but over a longer time period. The major spring species on the Au Sable River in Michigan is *B. lateralis*.

Hook Size: 16, 18, 20.
Larval Type: Humpless tube case-makers.

Species *Brachycentrus*

1. *B. numerosus* (Little Black Caddis) .... E M

Length: Male 8-10mm, female 11-12.5mm.
Color: Body dusky brownish-gray, almost black, with a wide green lateral line which becomes much darker as the insect ages, wings tawny with pale spots appearing light gray, legs and antennae paler than body.
Emergence: East, middle of April to end of May; Midwest first of May to last week of May.

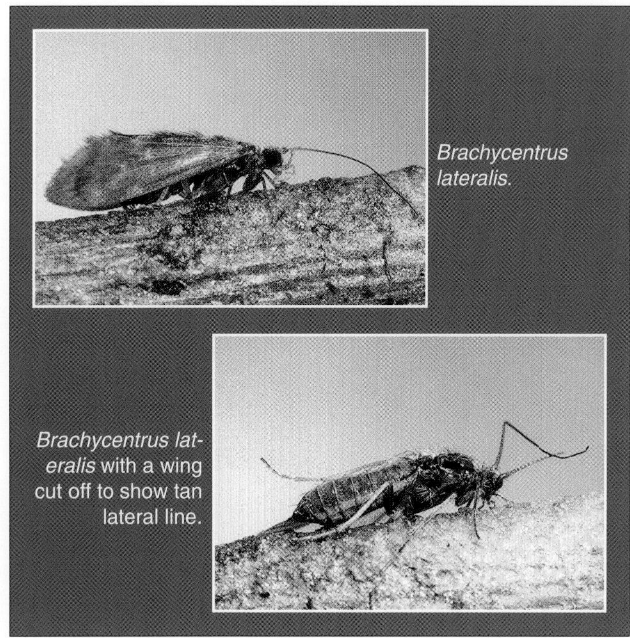

Brachycentrus lateralis.

Brachycentrus lateralis with a wing cut off to show tan lateral line.

2. *B. lateralis* .... E M

Length: Male 6-8mm, female 9-11mm.
Color: Males very similar to *B. numerosus*, abdominal lateral line tan.
Female: Body similar to *B. numerosus*, wings pale gray with a slightly darker anterior margin and a little tan mottling. They have an abdominal lateral line like males which is green. This is the big spring hatch in Michigan.
Emergence: Mid-April to end of May; earlier in the South.

3. *B. appalachia* .... E
Widespread from Nova Scotia to South Carolina.

Size: Male 7-8mm, female 8-10mm. New species as of 1984.
Color: Male body and appendages very dark gray, legs paler, wings gray with pale spots; female body straw colored, head and thorax dorsomesally darkened with a brownish tinge, forewing pale grayish. This is the only species of the group where the females have a different body color than the males.
Emergence: Starts in April in Georgia and May further North.

4. *B. occidentalis* W
From Wisconsin to Pacific Coast.

Size: Male 7-8mm, female 9-10mm.
Color: Grayish-brown, almost black, with an olive lateral line on the abdomen which becomes much darker as the insect ages, legs paler, forewings pale brownish-gray with black veins which make the wings look almost black.
Emergence: Mid-April to mid-June.

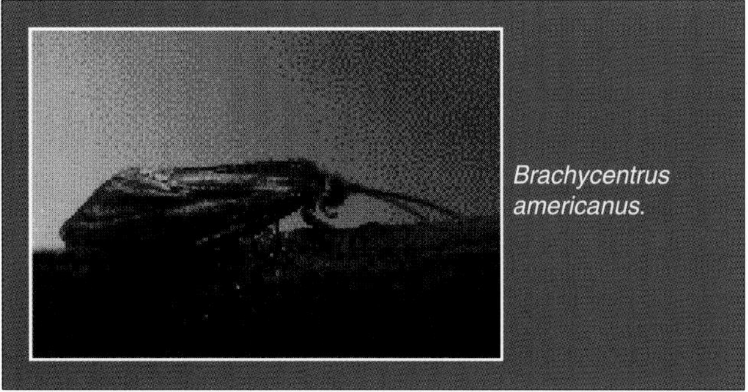
Brachycentrus americanus.

5. *B. americanus* E M W

Length: Male 7-10mm, female 11-13mm.
Color: Body brown, wings brown with extensive pale flecks, especially around the apex.
Emergence: Mid-July to first week of September in the West; Mid-May to Mid-July in the East.

6. *B. solomoni* E
From West Virginia to Quebec.

Length: Male 9-10mm, females 11-13mm. New species as of 1984.
Color: Body dark gray, tibia and tarsi paler, wings gray with paler spots in an indistinct subapical band.
Emergence: Mid-April to Mid-May.

There are seven other species of *Brachycentrus* of local importance to fishermen, they are: *B. nigrosoma* which is very similar to *B. numerosus* and is an Eastern species. *B. eco* is limited to California and Utah and is smaller, 5.5-8mm. *B. incanus* is an Eastern and Midwestern species, similar to *B. numerosus*. *B. fuliginosus* is quite rare, known only in northern Michigan and Canada. *B. chelatus* is a Southern species known from Alabama, Florida, Georgia and South Carolina. It is similar to *B. numerosus*. *B. spinae* is limited to the southern Appalachian region and is similar to *B. numerosus*. *B. etowahensis* is similar to *B. numerosus* and is limited to the southern end of the Appalachians.

Species *Micrasema* and *Amiocentrus*

1. *M. bactro* (Little Black Caddis, a k a Western Weedy Water Sedge) W
2. *A. asphilis* W

Length: 6-7.5mm.
Color: Black body with green lateral line, black wings, very dark gray legs, antennae gray with darker rings.
Emergence: Mid-July to early August on the Yellowstone, spring and late August to October on the Bighorn.

3. *M. rusticum* (Little Grannom) E M

Micrasema rusticum.

Length: 6-7.5mm.
Color: Very dark brown seeming black in life.
Emergence: Mid-May to late July in the late afternoon and evening.

Family Philopotamidae

Genera

Chimarra (Tiny Black Caddis)
Dolophilodes (Tiny Black Gold Speckled Wing Caddis) E M
(Medium Evening Sedge) W
Wormaldia (Little Autumn Sedge) E M W

Species *Chimarra*

These species' also come in spring at about the same time as *Brachycentrus* and often on the same day. *Chimarra* are noon emergers with ovipositing occuring in the afternoon. The pupae crawl out of the water and emerge on land. Females dive or crawl under water to lay their eggs. These are supposed to be common on the Au Sable River in Michigan, producing clouds of insects with heavy trout feeding. We have not found it important in the Midwest or anywhere else. The insect that anglers have been calling *Chimarra* is *B. lateralis*.

Hook Size: 20-22.
Larval Type: Fingernet caddisflies.

Species *Chimarra*

1. *C. aterrima* (Tiny Black Caddis). Common in the Midwest. E M
2. *C. obscura.* Common in Southern tailwaters. E M
3. *C. socia.* Common in the Northeast. E

Length: 6-8mm.
Color: Body very dark brown, almost black, sides of abdomen and parts of femora white, with black wings, antennae and legs dark brown.
Emergence: First of May to mid-June often mixed with *Brachycentrus.*

Species *Dolophilodes*

The pupae of *D. distinctus* emerge midstream and crawl over the surface of the water to shore, at least in the spring. The females are wingless in winter and spring. When fishing to an emergence, adult and emerger imitations are useless. The angler must use a hackled pupa which should be skated over the water toward shore. The egg-laying flight is important for both species. Later in the summer pupae swim or crawl to shore, or emerge in the stream.

Size: *D. aequalis,* sizes 16-20. Individuals become smaller as season progresses.
D. distinctus, sizes 20-22.

1. *D. aequalis* (Medium Evening Sedge) W
   Common in Montana in small streams and rivers such as Rock Creek.
2. *D. distinctus* (Tiny Gold Flecked Wing Sedge) E M
   Common in Michigan from April to fall. Widespread from Northeast to North Carolina, prefers cold streams.

Dolophilodes distinctus.

Length: *D. aequalis* variable, 12mm to 7mm.
D. distinctus, 8mm.
Color: *D. aequalis*, earlier in the season dark, almost black, becoming lighter (light brown) and smaller. *D. distinctus* is very dark brownish-gray, wings have small gold spots or scales, legs and antennae almost black.
Emergence: *D. aequalis* most important during evenings in July. *D. distinctus* year-round, winter females are wingless, midsummer evening emergers have wings. In spring there is a transition period where some have wings and some do not. This period occurs in late April and early June just before and during the Hendrickson and Grannom hatches and the emergence is morning and afternoon. Does not come in large numbers but emerges almost everyday during the entire season.

Species *Wormaldia*

These insects are most common in cold trout streams and uncommon in tailwaters and spring creeks.

1. *W. anilla* (Little Autumn Sedge). Common in small streams in the Northwest. W
2. *W. gabriella.* Found in larger streams than *anilla.* W
3. *W. moesta.* Widespread in the East and Midwest. E M

Length: 8-10mm.
Color: Body olive brown, wings gray, some Western species mottled brown, legs brown.
Emergence: *W. anilla,* April to June and September to November. *W. gabriella,* August to October. *W. moesta,* March and April.

Family Leptoceridae

Genera

Oecetis (Long-Horned Sedge)
Ceraclea (Dark Brown Scaly Wing Sedge)
Nectopsyche (White Miller)
Mystacides (Black Dancer)

The species' of this family are summer fliers. They have very long antennae, two and one half times the length of their bodies. The wings are slimmer than most caddis and the bodies are shorter and slimmer in relation to the length of their wings. The pupae crawl or swim to the surface to emerge and sprawl on the surface or dive under water to lay their eggs. Emergence is in the afternoon and evening except for the White Miller which emerges just after dark, and the Black Dancer which emerges in the morning in the West.

Hook Sizes:
Oecetis: 14-16
Ceraclea: 16-18-20
Nectopsyche: 14-16
Mystacides: 18-20
Larval Type: Long-horned case-makers.

Species *Oecetis*

1. *O. disjunctiva* (Gray Wing Long-Horned Sedge) W

Length: 11-12mm.
Color: Males have bright blue-green bodies while the females are a golden yellow. The wings are light gray and the legs and antennae are tan, the antennae show conspicuous darker rings.
Emergence: Early June to late July in the evening.

2. *O. avara* (Tan Spotted Wing Long-Horned Sedge)..E M W

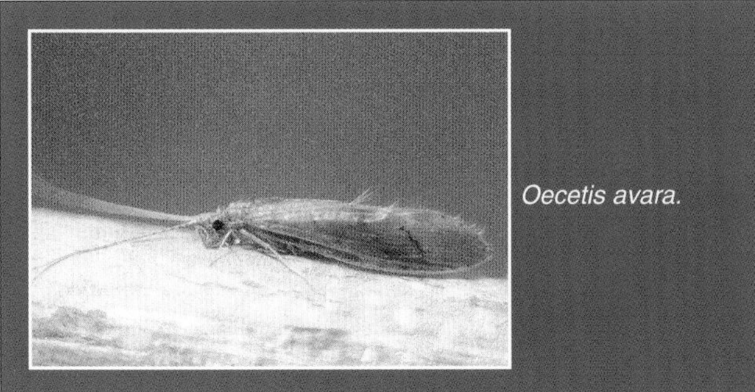
Oecetis avara.

Length: 11-12mm.
Color: Bodies are yellowish-olive to tan, wings light brown with dark brown or black dots. Legs and antennae ginger, antennae with conspicuous darker rings.
Emergence: June to early September.

3. *O. inconspicua* (Plain Red-Brown Long-Horned Sedge)..E M

Length: 10-12mm.
Color: Body light brown, wings reddish-brown without distinct markings, legs and antennae tan, antennae with darker stripes.
Emergence: Early May to early October.

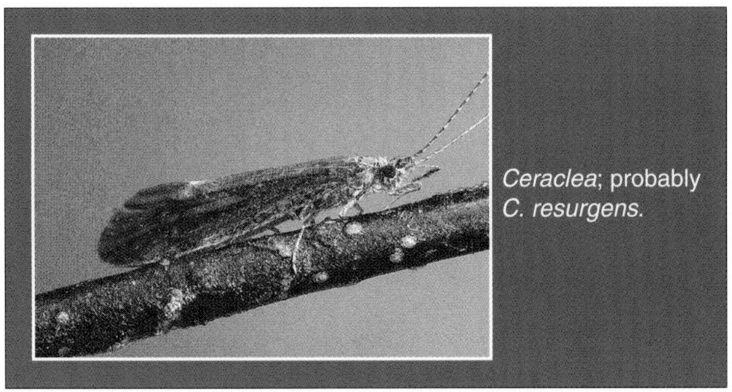
Ceraclea; probably *C. resurgens.*

Species *Ceraclea*

1. *C. transversa* (Plain Brown Scaly Wing Sedge)..E M

Length: 11-13mm.
Color: Various shades of reddish-brown from light to dark with scarcely any markings except darker rings on antennae.
Emergence: Late June to late August.

Ceraclea transversa.

2. *C. arielles* (Plain Brown Scaly Wing)........................M

Length: 11-12mm.
Color: Very similar to *C. transversa*, most common species of the genus on the Au Sable River.
Emergence: June to late August.

Many other species dark brown to black with dark wings with light scales, such as *C. tarsi-punctatus, C. alagnus* which are common in the Midwest.

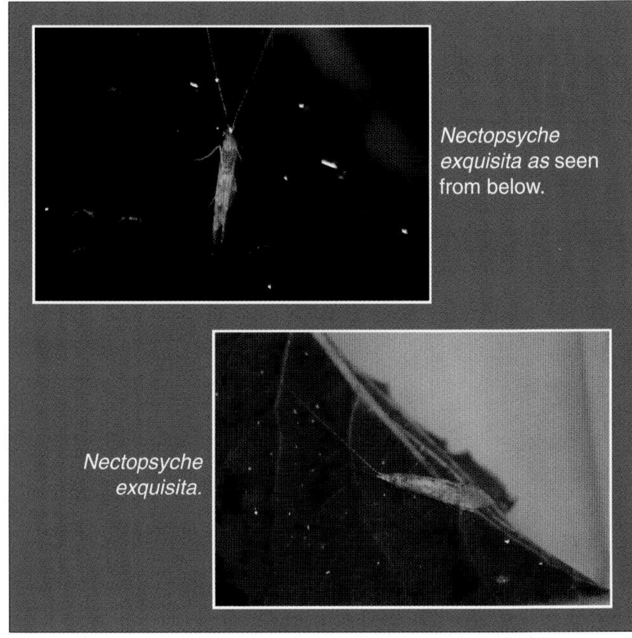
Nectopsyche exquisita as seen from below.

Nectopsyche exquisita.

Species *Nectopsyche*

1. *N. albida* and *exquisita* (White Miller)..................E M

Length: 11-16mm.
Color: Body is greenish with a little yellow, wings are cream with some obscure tan markings. Legs are tan and antennae are cream with brown rings.

Emergence: Last of July to third week in September after dark. Trout will take adult imitations at dusk.

Species *Mystacides*

1. *M. alafimbriata* (Black Dancer)........W

Length: 8-9mm.
Color: Body dark green to black to dull amber depending on river. Wings black, legs dark gray, antennae gray with black wings.
Emergence: Mid-July to late August from 7:00 a.m. to 10:00 a.m. on slow-moving rivers. Adults ride the water for a long time in the morning.

2. *M. sepulchralis*........E M W

Mystacides sepulchralis.

Length: 8-9mm.
Color: Shiny blue-black, wings and thorax have a metallic sheen.
Emergence: Late May to September from lakes and slow-moving rivers, morning and evening.

3. M. *longicornis=interjecta*........E M W

Length: 8-9mm.
Color: Rusty brown, wings cloaked with golden hair arranged to form golden and brown bands.
Emergence: Mid-June to late August from lakes and slow-moving rivers morning and evening.

Family Helicopsychidae

Genera *Helicopsyche* (Speckled Peter)

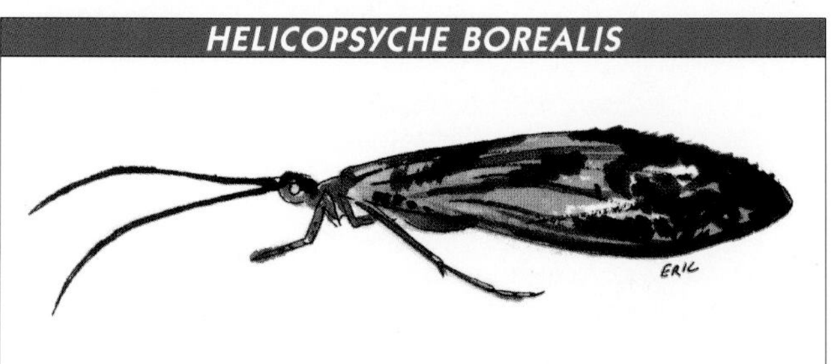

The emergence and egg laying of these small caddis occurs in the evening. During egg laying the females float to the surface close to the banks, crawl under water and flop on the surface to oviposit, then they ride the water serenely in their normal resting position where trout take them with gentle rises.

Hook Size: 20-22.
Larval Type: Snail case-makers.

Species *Helicopsyche*

1. *H. borealis* (Speckled Peter)........E M W

Length: 5-7mm.
Color: Body is bright amber, wings light brown with heavy speckling of dark brown giving the appearance of a very dark gray-brown when in the hand; legs and antennae straw yellow.
Emergence: Mid-June to early July in the West and early May to a June peak in the East and Midwest.

Family Glossosomatidae

Genera

Glossosoma (Little Black Short-Horned Sedge)
Protoptila (*Pseudo* Microcaddis)

These caddis are morning emergers in early spring and evening fliers as the season progresses. The emergence is usually more important than the egg laying. Females dive under water to oviposit, pupae swim to the surface to emerge, at least some pupae swim to the surface and swim on the surface to shore where they take about two minutes to crawl out of their pupal shuck.

Hook Sizes: *Glossosoma:* 20-24.
Protoptila: 24-28.
Larval Type: Saddle case-maker.

Species *Glossosoma*

1. *G. nigrior* (Little Black Short-Horned Sedge)........E M W
2. *G. intermedium*........E M W
3. *G. montana*........W

Glossosoma nigrior.

Length: 6-10mm.
Color: Body, wings and appendages grayish-black, wings of *G. nigrior* have golden flecks and body has a lighter brown side and darker gray-brown dorsal and ventral. Wings of *G. montana* have tan speckling. Some other species of this family are reported as tan and brown. The adults resemble *Rhyacophila* but are smaller.
Emergence: Late April to late June in the East and Midwest, and the last of May to September in the West in the evening. There is a continual emergence of adults from spring to early fall from cold running streams in the evening. Worms drift as they leave their cases to build larger ones. *G. nigrior* may be another species anglers on the Au Sable River in Michigan call *Chimarra,* as they start emerging in the spring when *Chimarra* are supposed to hatch. *Chimarra* are present but do not appear to be important.

Species *Protoptila*

Black Protoptila.
Oecetis avara.

These are very small forms which have many species and can come in almost any color. They are between 2.5 to 5.5mm long and can be important even though they are tiny, because they often emerge in huge numbers. The most common colors in the rivers we fish are either all black or a gray wing with a cinnamon body *(p. immaculata)*. They emerge mainly in midsummer.

Family Lepidostomidae

Genus *Lepidostoma*
(Little Gray Sedge, Little Black Sedge)

These caddis are evening emergers and egg layers. Pupae swim to the surface to emerge. The emergers ride the water for longer than most caddis and pupae, emergers and adults will take fish. Adults ride the water quietly during egg laying. There are more than 25 species in the Nearctic region but their distribution is very localized. This genus has been called the Little Plain Brown Sedge and is described as having a plain brown wing and a brown body, but the two most important species (at least to us), *L. pluviale* and *L. togatum*, have green or olive bodies. *L. togatum* and *L. sommermanae* (Ohio) have two black spots on a gray wing. We have not seen any totally brown species, but it is entirely possible that there are some.

Hook Size: 18-20.
Larval Type: Tube case-makers.

Lepidostoma togatum.

Species *Lepidostoma*

1. *L. pluviale* (Little Gray Sedge, Little Black Sedge) .... W
2. *L. togatum* .... E M
3. *L. costalis* .... EM
4. *L. bryanti* .... M
5. *L. sommermanae (*Ohio)
6. *L. coastlias* .... E M
7. *L. strophis* .... E M W

Size: 9-11mm.
Color: Body, olive or green with a darker dorsum. Wings grayish-brown or grayish, some species have patches of hair which may be light or dark and look spotted or patterned. Legs and antennae grayish-brown, antennae have dark bands. Some males (*L. pluviale*) have a distinct dark gray recurve on the top of their wings which can be used for identification.
Emergence: Mid-June to late September in evening in the West. Last of June to mid-August in the East and Midwest, some may come in the morning. They inhabit small, cool woodland streams. Adults ride the surface for a long time at emergence, so trout will take pupae and adults, and dry adults at egg laying. In the Midwest *L. bryanti* begins in June, followed by *L. costalis* in late July and then *L. togatum* in August to September.

Family Psychomyiidae

Genera

Psychomyia (Dinky Purple-Breasted Sedge)
Lype (Dark Eastern Woodland Sedge)

The pupae of these Trichoptera swim to the surface to emerge in the river. The females dive under water to oviposit. The Eastern Woodland Sedge flies in the afternoon and females start egg laying in the early evening. The Purple-Breasted Sedge emerges just at dark except on overcast days when it can occur at any time.

Hook Size: 20-22.
Larval Type: Nettube caddisflies.

Species *Psychomyia*

1. *P. flavida* (Dinky Purple-Breasted Sedge)............E M W

Size: 5-6mm.
Color: Body yellow with a purple cast, wings brown, antennae and legs yellow.
Emergence: June to August usually after dark.

Species *Lype*

1. *L. diversa* (Dark Eastern Woodland Sedge).........E M

Size: 6-7mm.
Color: Body very dark brown, wings uniformly a very dark gray, almost black, legs and antennae very dark brown.
Emergence: May and June in afternoon and evening from small, cool woodland streams.

Family Rhyacophilidae

Genus *Rhyacophila* (Green Sedge)

The bright green larvae of this caddis are usually more important to trout fishermen than the adults. The family is widespread and abundant, but on some rivers they sometimes do not emerge in a coordinated fashion to cause selective feeding by the fish. The larvae on the other hand are free-living, of good size and readily available to trout all season long. These are fast-water caddis, the larvae live in rapids and riffles and the adults emerge and oviposit in the same riffles. The pupae are fast emergers, the females enter the water to lay their eggs. Some individuals of this genera run to shore after emergence so a dry fly skittered from the riffles to shore can be effective.

Hook Size: 14-18. A few species are larger.
Larval Type: Free-living worms.

Species *Rhyacophila*

1. *R. bifila*..........W
2. *R. coloradensis*..........W
3. *R. melita* (Au Sable River)
4. *R. manistee*..........E M
5. *R. fuscula*..........E M
6. *R. vuphipes*..........S
7. *R.* species (many other species similar in appearance)

Rhyacophila melita showing green body.

Rhyacophila larva.

Length: Up to 18mm, but most species 8-13mm.
Color: Body green, wings mottled light and dark gray and brown, legs ginger, antennae gray with darker rings.
Emergence: April through October in the west; May to July in the East and Midwest.

Family Hydroptilidae (True Microcaddis)

Genera

Agraylea (Salt and Pepper Microcaddis)
Hydroptila (Vari-Colored Microcaddis)
Leucotrichia (Ring-Horned Microcaddis)
Oxyethira (Cream and Brown Microcaddis)

HYDROPTILA HAMATA

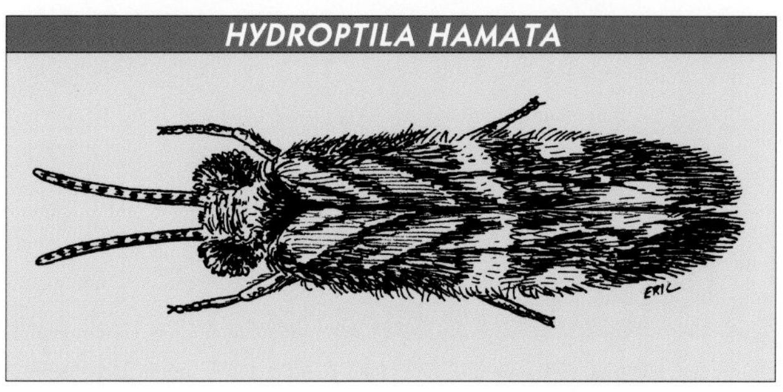

These are very small caddisflies, generally from 2 to 5mm (sizes 24-36) which is why we do not list them in the true super hatch category, however they can be important at times and do create selective feeding when they are on the water in great numbers. They are more important on slow rivers and gentle spring creeks where trout can sip them without expending much energy. The pupae swim or crawl to the surface, the females dive or crawl under water to lay their eggs.

Hook Size: 24-36.
Larval Type: Purse case-makers.

Species *Agraylea*

1. *A. multipunctata* (Salt and Pepper Microcaddis)........E M W

Length: 4-5mm.
Color: Body green, wings black and white mottled to almost black, legs and antennae black.
Emergence: June and July at dawn.

Species *Hydroptila*

1. *H.* species (about 60 species) (Vari-Colored Microcaddis)........E M W

Length: 3-4mm.
Color: Bodies can be almost any color, wings gray to brown. Can be spotted or unspotted, legs and antennae tan to black. Colors vary even in the same species.
Emergence: All summer any time of day.

Species *Leucotrichia*

1. *L. pictipes* (Ring-Horned Microcaddis)........E M W

Length: 4-4.5mm.
Color: Body and appendages dark brown to black, antennae and tarsi banded with white, wings with a few scattered light spots.
Emergence: Summer, usually at midday.

Species *Oxyethira*

1. *O. michiganensis, serrata, pallida* (Cream and Brown Microcaddis)........E M W

Length: 2-3mm.
Color: Body greenish-yellow, wings cream and brown mottled, antennae and legs yellow.
Emergence: Summer, usually evenings.

Family Molannidae

Genus *Molanna* (Gray Checkered Sedge)

Two species of this family are important to trout fishermen both of which are found in the East and Midwest.

MOLANNA BLENDA

The pupae swim to the surface to emerge, the females crawl or dive under water to oviposit and prefer quiet streams. The pupae take a long time to cast their shucks.

Size: 14-16.
Larval Type: Hood case-makers.

Species *Molanna*

1. *M. tryphena* (Gray Checkered Sedge)........E M
2. *M. uniophila*........E M

Size: 15-16mm.
Color: Body brown, wings gray with a mottled checkered pattern of light and dark areas mostly in the middle, legs and antennae brown.
Emergence: Mid-May to early September.

Family Phryganeidae

Genera

Phryganea (Rush Sedge)
Ptilostomis (Giant Rusty Sedge)

The large pupae crawl or swim to the bank to emerge on shore. Females lay their eggs on the water's surface but run across the surface of the water to return to shore. These are large insects so they attract large trout to feed. Fishing tactics are different from most other Trichoptera, the pupae should be crawled to shore in quiet backwaters. The adult imitations should be skittered to shore during ovipositing. The egg-laying flights are in the evening. They prefer quiet streams and lakes.

Hook Size: 10-12.
Larval Type: Giant case-makers.

Species *Phryganea*

1. *P. cinerea* (Rush Sedge)........E M W
2. *P. sayi*........E M

PHRYGANEA CINERA

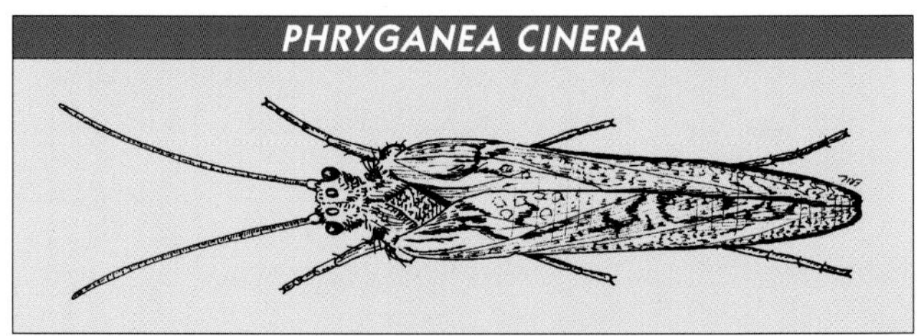

PHRYGANEA SAYI

Size: 21-25mm.
Color: Body reddish-brown, wings gray and brown with an irregular pattern of shades of brown with light gray patches along the posterior margin. These form triangular marks when the wings are folded. Legs and antennae yellow to brown.
Emergence: May and June (*P. sayi* two weeks later than *P. cinerea*).

Species *Ptilostomis*

1. *P. ocellifera* (Giant Rusty Sedge) E M W
2. *P. semifasciata* E M W

PTILOSTOMIS OCELLIFERA

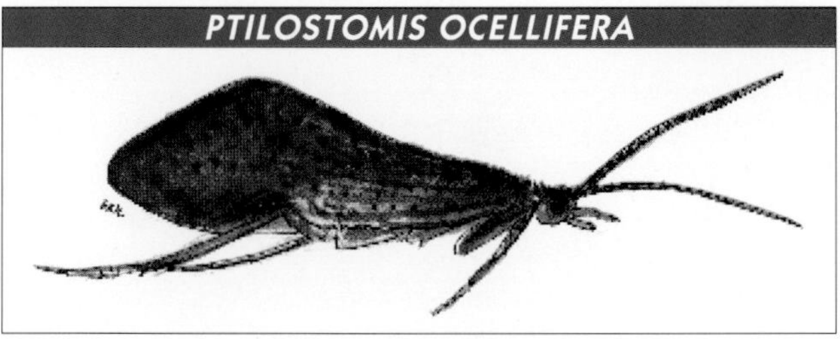

Size: 21-25mm.
Color: Yellowish-brown, wing light reddish-brown with some irregular and obscure darker markings, legs light reddish-brown, antennae darker reddish-brown with dark rings.
Emergence: June and July after dark from lakes and slow weedy streams.

Family Odontoceridae

Genus *Psilotreta* (Dark Blue Sedge)

The pupae of this family swim and crawl to the surface to emerge, females drop on the surface of the stream where they flop and flutter while extruding their egg mass. The emergence and egg laying take place in the evening.

Hook Size: 14-16.
Larval Type: Strong case-makers.

Species *Psilotreta*

1. *P. labia, frontalis* (Dark Blue Sedge) E
2. *P. labia* E

PSILOTRETA LABIA

Size: 12-14mm.
Color: Body green or almost black with legs and mouth parts showing lighter areas of grayish-brown, wings very dark grayish-brown with very small, irregularly scattered lighter dots. Legs and antennae almost black.
Emergence: Late May to Mid-June in the evening. (*P. frontalis* inhabits smaller streams, there is some overlap however.)

Family Polycentropidae

Genera

Polycentropus (Brown Checkered Summer Sedge)
Nyctiophylax (Dinky Light Summer Sedge)

These caddis live in the quieter areas of streams. The pupae swim to the surface to emerge in the evening during summer. Females swim to the bottom of the stream to oviposit.

Hook Size: 18-20.
Larval Type: Trumpetnet and tube-making caddisflies.

Species *Polycentropus*

1. *P. cinereus* (Brown Checkered Summer Sedge) E M W

Size: 7-9mm.
Color: Body yellowish-brown to brown, wings light and dark brown mottling, legs and antennae brown.
Emergence: Mid-June to Mid-July, much more common in lakes than streams in Michigan.

Species *Nyctiophylax*

1. *N. moestus* (Dinky Light Summer Sedge) E M W

Size: 22-24, 5-7mm.
Color: Body yellow-brown, wings brown, legs and antennae yellowish-brown.
Emergence: Late afternoon and evening in June, egg laying and emergence take place at the same time.

Family Limnephilidae

Genera

Limnephilus (Summer Flier Sedge)
Apatania (Early Smoky Wing Sedge)
Frenesia (Dot Wing Sedge)
Goera (Little Gray Sedge)
Neophylax (Little Dot Wing Sedge)
Pycnopsyche (Great Brown Autumn Sedge)
Dicosmoecus (Giant Orange Sedge)
Hesperophylax (Silver Striped Sedge)
Hydratophylax (Giant Cream-Patterned Wing Sedge)
Platycentropus (Chocolate and Cream Sedge)

This family is very diverse. It has species of all sizes and comes in a great variety of colors. The habits of the various genera are also diverse so it must be handled a little differently from the other families. We will explain some of the habits under the genera listings rather than the family listings.

Emergence is accomplished by swimming to the surface or crawling to shore, egg laying is by diving or crawling under water in most of the species but about one half of the subfamily Limnephilidae lay their eggs on shoreside objects; but even here some individuals may crawl under water.

Hook Size: 22-24.
Larval Type: Tube case-makers.

Genus *Limnephilus* (Summer Flier)

When the adults emerge in spring they are not sexually mature, they mature and oviposit in the fall. Females lay eggs on objects near the water or crawl into the water. Some species have two generations each year.

Hook Size: 14-16.

Species *Limnephilus*

1. *L. sericeus* .... E M W
2. *L. submonilifer* (Summer Flier) .... E M
3. *L. thorus* .... W

LIMNEPHILUS INDIVISUS

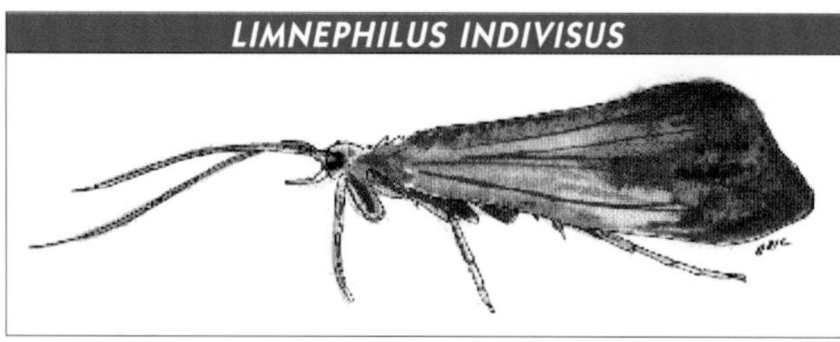

Length: 13-16mm.
Color: Body brown to brownish-olive and slender with a darker dorsum, wings brown, variegated with irregular light and darker spots, legs and antennae tan to brown.
Emergence: Mid-April to mid-June, sometimes has two generations each year, one in spring and one in fall. *L. thorus* emerges from the Bighorn in Montana in large numbers in the fall, during September and October. It comes in late evening and after dark. It is 17-19mm long with a cinnamon brown body; females have an olive overtone. Legs and antennae are cinnamon brown and wings are tan with three brown marks in the upper middle area, a thin dark line along the top and a transparent line below the three brown marks.

Genus *Apatania* (Early Smoky Wing Sedge)

This is a very important Trichoptera in southern New England. Emergence and egg laying occur all day in the spring.

Hook Size: 18-20.

Species *Apatania*

1. *A. incerta* (Early Smoky Wing Sedge) .... E

Length: 7-8.5mm.
Color: Body grayish-brown, wing smoky gray, legs and antennae grayish-brown.
Emergence: Mid-April to late May during the day.

Genus *Frenesia* (Dot Wing Sedge)

These caddisflies emerge late in the season in the East and Midwest. They are very important in November and December, they continue through February, especially on unseasonally warm days. Pupae crawl and swim to the shallows to emerge in late morning and afternoon. Egg-laying is probably near shore. They are especially important as not much else is hatching at these times.

Hook Size: *F. missa,* 16-18; *F. difficilis,* 14-16.

Species *Frenesia*

1. *F. missa* (Dot Wing Sedge) .... E M
2. *F. difficilis* .... E

FRENESIA MISSA

Length: *F. missa*, 11-13mm; *F. difficilis*, 14.5-15.5mm.
Color: Body dark grayish-brown with a light yellowish lateral line, wings brown with uniform tan translucent dots, legs ginger, antennae light brown.
Emergence: November and December on warm afternoons.

Genus *Goera* (Little Gray Sedge)

These little caddis emerge from riffles. *G. stylata* is found in the Midwest.

GOERA CALCARATA

Hook Size: 18.

Species *Goera*

1. *G. stylata* (Little Gray Sedge) M
2. *G. calcarata* E M W

Length: 8-10mm.
Color: Body pale yellow, wings tannish-gray, legs tannish-gray, antennae dark gray.
Emergence: Late May to early June from small, cold, gravel-bottomed streams.

Genus *Neophylax*

The pupae of this genera emerge in the daytime and oviposit in the afternoon in fall. *N. fuscous* emerges in large numbers on the Rogue and Muskegon rivers in Michigan.

NEOPHYLAX AUTUMNUS

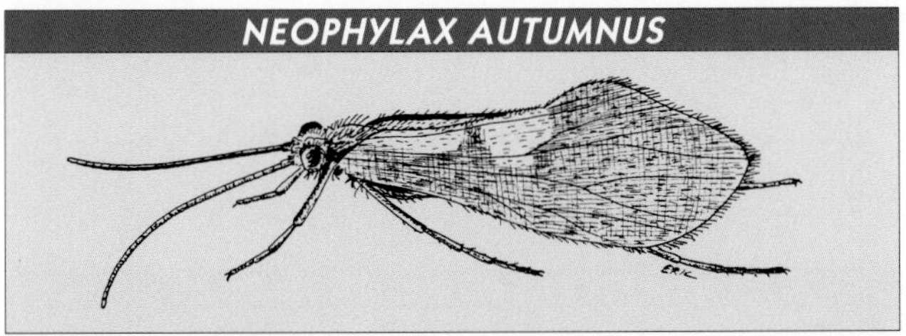

Neophylax fuscous.

Species *Neophylax*

Some species in this genus have been moved to the family Uenoidae, including *N. concinnus* and *N. fuscous*.

1. *U. concinnus=autumnus* (Autumn Mottled Sedge, a k a Little Dot Wing Sedge) E M
2. *N. rickeri* W
3. *N. splendens* W
4. *U. fuscous* M

Length: *N. concinnus* 9-12mm; *N. rickeri* and *N. splendens* 16-18mm; *N. fuscous* 9-11.3mm.
Color: Body brownish-yellow to dark grayish-brown, *N. fuscous* with yellowish lateral line, wings mottled light and dark brown; *N. concinnus* has a light brown double diamond design. Legs and antennae brownish-yellow.

Genus *Pycnopsyche* (Great Brown Autumn Sedge)

The pupae emerge and adults oviposit mostly at night but some activity occurs at dusk and dawn. Large trout are on the lookout for this meaty insect. Pupae migrate to the banks to emerge and then crawl under water to lay their eggs. A large pupal imitation is effective when fished slowly on the bottom. *P. guttifer* is supposed to be rare in the West, but the Bighorn River in Montana has a good population and imitations produce big fish in September and October. This is also a big fish producer on the Muskegon River in Michigan during October.

Hook Size: 12-14.

Species *Pycnopsyche*

1. *P. guttifer* (Great Brown Autumn Sedge) E M W
2. *P. lepida* E M
3. *P. scabripennis* E M

PYCNOPSYCHE GUTTIFER

Pycnopsyche guttifer.

Length: 19-22mm.
Color: Body cinnamon, wings yellow to brown with two conspicuous brownish-black marks in the middle and a black border at the apex. Legs and antennae cinnamon, antennae with dark bands.
Emergence: Mid-July to October.

Genus *Dicosmoecus* (Giant Orange Sedge)

The larvae, pupae and adults are all important stages of this huge caddisfly. The larvae exhibit behavioral drift in summer and unlike most aquatic insects, the drift is in the afternoon. Pupae migrate to the shallows before emerging in late afternoon and evening. Egg-laying takes place at dusk and females make a commotion which the fish notice. Fishing a pupa and a dry on a dropper in the shallows with a twitching retrieve can be deadly.

Hook Size: 4-8.

Species *Dicosmoecus* (Giant Orange Sedge)

1. *D. atripes*.......W
2. *D. gilvipes*.......W
3. *D. jucundus*.......W

Length: 18-30mm.
Color: Body orange, wing gray and brown mottled with heavy veins, antennae and legs tan.
Emergence: September and October.

Genus *Hesperophylax* (Silver Striped Sedge)

These insects emerge at night. They are so large, trout are on the lookout for this summer emerger.

Hook Size: 12 for *H. designatus*; 6-8 for *H. incisus*.

Species *Hesperophylax*

1. *H. designatus* (Silver Striped Sedge).......E M
2. *H. incisus*.......E M W

HESPEROPHYLAX DESIGNATUS

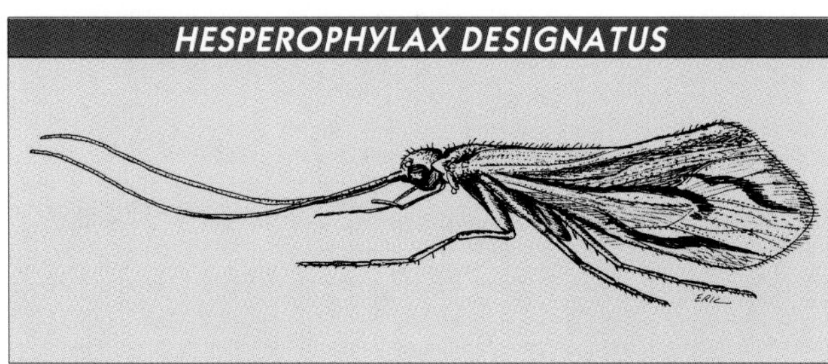

Length: 17-20mm Eastern species; 30-34mm Western species.
Color: Body yellow to cinnamon, wings cream and light brown with a long silver stripe, legs and antennae ginger.
Emergence: Midsummer.

Genus *Hydratophylax*
(Giant Cream-Patterned Wing Sedge)

These caddis emerge in the morning and trout feed mostly on the pupae, egg-laying is not important to fishermen.

Hook Size: 4-6.

Species *Hydratophylax*

1. *H. argus* (Giant Cream-Patterned Wing Sedge).......E M
2. *H. hesperus*.......W

HYDRATOPHYLAX ARGUS

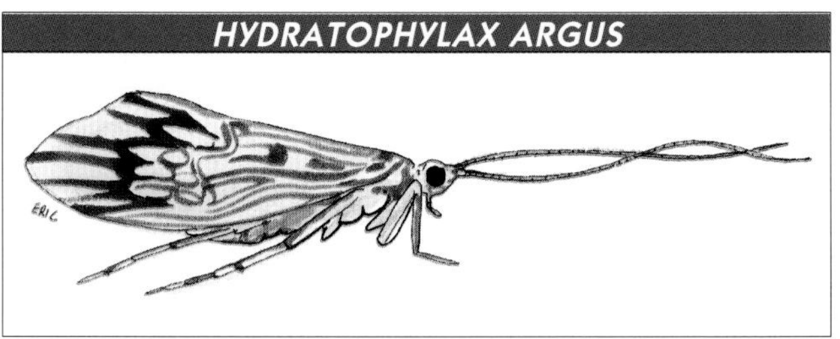

Length: 30-34mm.
Color: Body yellowish-tan, wing light brown with cream patterns, *H. argus* has a "Z" pattern. Head yellow, antennae dark grayish-brown, legs tannish.
Emergence: Late May to fall for Eastern species; August to October for Western species.

Genus *Platycentropus*
(Chocolate and Cream Sedge)

These large caddis are nocturnal emergers in midsummer, but some big trout can be taken early in the morning on dry adult patterns.

Hook Size: 12-14.

Species *Platycentropus*

1. *P. radiatus* (Chocolate and Cream Sedge).......E M

PLATYCENTROPUS RADIATUS

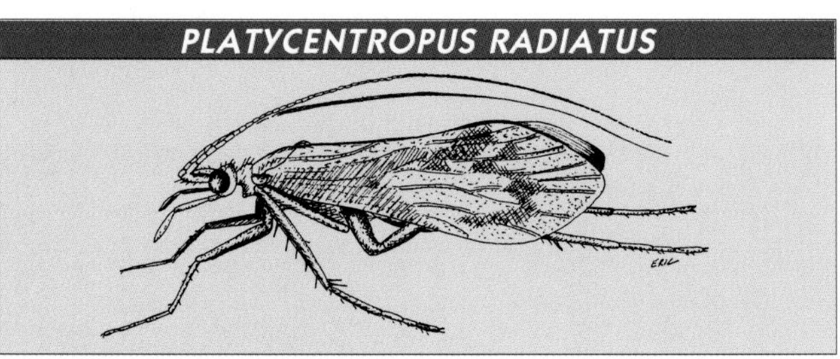

Length: 20-23mm.
Color: Body yellow to brown, wings shades of cream to dark brown, legs and antennae dark yellow.
Emergence: July and August.

Chapter VI

COLLECTING AND IDENTIFYING CADDISFLIES

We have provided some easy ways of identifying caddisflies, in many cases to the species level. In the few instances where identifying the insect to the species level is extremely difficult, like with the *Hydropsyche*, even for professional biologists, it is usually not necessary because they look and act alike. The tier could not tie a pattern for one species and a different pattern for another species even if he wanted to. Other than some variation in body color which can vary from stream to stream, even in the same species, all the species of *Hydropsyche* are very similar. Their emerging and egg-laying habits are also similar, so angling methods for all *Hydropsyche* species are the same.

The first method of identification is a key we call the "Fishermen's Key To Caddisflies". There are three separate keys, one for the East, one for the Midwest and one for the West. These are keys for the most common caddisflies which can cause intensive and selective feeding by trout in running water. They include many species reported to be significant other than those on the super hatch list, and may be important in areas we have not fished. With these keys the fisherman need only measure the length of the insect from head to wing tip, note the color of the body and length of antennae. The angler can then go down the keys to the correct length and color, note the number at the end of that line, go to that numbered line and compare the descriptions under that section.

The family, genus and quite often the exact species, can be easily discovered. All this without the use of any magnification. The peak emergence is also listed, so if similar appearing species are in the same key number section, taking the timing of the hatch into consideration will usually clear up any confusion.

When the family of the insect is known it is even easier to determine exactly which natural you are fishing to by using the "Fishermen's Key To Caddisflies". Because of this, we have included a scientific key to the families which can be used for positive identification. This key is also very easy to use but the use of a microscope is usually necessary, although sometimes a 10x slide magnifier will suffice. A 30x and a 100x microscope can be obtained from Radio Shack for less than fifteen dollars.

This key was taken from entomology texts and modified by us to make it easier to use. We eliminated the rare families not usually found on trout streams in numbers enough to cause selective feeding by fish. With a little practice, the angler can quickly determine the family of the insect and be sure of its determination.

Scientific keys for some genera and species are also included. These are for the most important groups which are truly the super caddisflies. Personally we get a lot of enjoyment out of collecting and identifying the insects, and with a little practice, the scientific keys are not that difficult, with

one exception. When the keys to the species require the comparison of male genitalia, identification does become difficult. Fortunately some keys also include female genitalia which are much easier. Some keys to the species compare wing patterns, these are very simple to use. The main piece of equipment needed for using the scientific keys is a low-power, binocular, dissecting microscope.

Collecting Caddisflies

For collecting naturals we use a long-handled fine mesh net called a sweep net. With this you can sweep bushes, tree branches and the grass along river banks. You can also swoop flying caddisflies from the air. A small aquarium net can be carried to capture floating insects while fishing. The easiest collection method is the use of a light trap. This consists of a portable fluorescent light which can be obtained from any sporting goods store which carries camping equipment. A little alcohol is placed in a white pan and the light is placed near it. The insects are attracted to the light, get into the alcohol and are trapped. This method has the advantage of collecting insects while you are elsewhere.

LONG-HANDLED NET

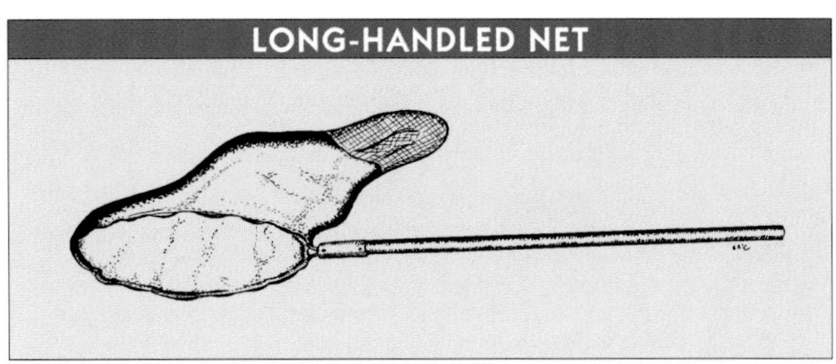

A good preserving medium is 80 percent grain alcohol or isopropyl alcohol with a little acetic acid added. The insects can be stored in small bottles which should be labeled with the date, river and county they were collected from. The vials should be completely filled with alcohol and some cotton inserted into the neck of the vial before the top is placed on. This keeps the specimens from knocking around in the bottle. Good field notes should be taken while the insects are alive. They usually change color quickly when immersed in the preservative and without records you will not be able to replicate the correct shades when dressing imitations. Sometimes it is desirable to store adult caddisflies in a dry state. These are mounted on insect pins and stored in a standard mounting box with a glass top.

Rearing Caddisflies

Larvae and cased pupae can be collected from the river bottom, transferred to an iced cooler, transported home, transferred to an aquarium and reared to adulthood. When collecting pupae which are still in cases, care must be taken when separating them from rocks or logs. They are easily damaged so use a sharp, thin knife to collect them from underwater objects. The best way to transfer cased pupae is to take the whole rock home in a cooler. Net-building caddisfly larvae and free-living larvae can be seined from riffles.

AQUARIUM SET-UP FOR REARING CADDIS

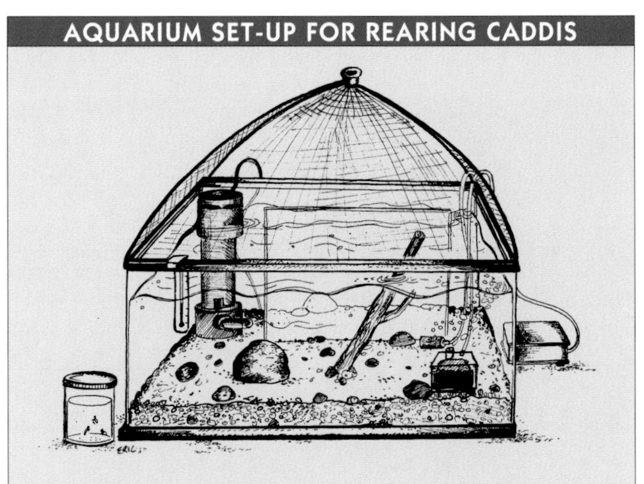

Clearing Technique

If you wish to study adult insects and take the study to the species level, accurate identification for many species must be based on characteristics of the male and female genitalia. It is usually necessary to clear the genitalia to see the diagnostic characters. For this we use Potassium Hydroxide (KOH), (caustic soda). Remove the apical 1/3 of the abdomen and place it in a 10 to 15 percent solution of the liquid. Allow it to soak for 6-12 hours, then place it in a dish of distilled water. In a few minutes the specimen should soften up. Gently press the abdomen until the dissolved viscera has been worked out of the shell. Transfer the specimen through three baths of distilled water, leaving it three or more hours in each. Then place it in a dish of alcohol with a few drops of acetic acid. Remove the preparation to neutral alcohol. It is now ready to study. If it did not soften after the 6-12 hour soaking, resoak it in a five percent solution of KOH for five or 10 minutes then squeeze out the viscera. Prepare a hot treatment by placing the solution in a vial and place it in a beaker of water. A little twisted wire should be placed in the beaker so the vial does not touch the bottom. Heat the beaker till the water boils, the caustic solution will not boil. Then go through the procedures described earlier.

A compound microscope may be needed for this study although some modern dissecting microscopes are powerful enough for the purpose. The cleared genitalia can be placed in pure glycerine for study. A slide with a ground-out place in which the glycerine is placed can be convenient for study. The terms commonly used in the keys are illustrated in the drawings in Chapter VII.

Identifying Larvae

A very good way to anticipate a caddis emergence is to examine the rocks and logs on the bottom of a river and sein the gravel. The seine will get the free-living worms which are *Rhyacophila*. These are only found in cold, fast-flowing streams. It will also capture the netspinners, trumpetnet and tube-making caddisflies (Family Polycentropodidae), and the most important of all, the common netspinners. These are of the Family Hydropsychidae. Three of the genera in this family produce the best and longest hatches and the best dry-fly fishing. Although these netspinners live in the net and have a little silken retreat nearby, they will be dislodged when gravel is disturbed so they will show up in the seine.

Case-making caddisflies usually do not show up in the seine, especially if they have attached the case to a rock or a log which they do just before pupation. These must be collected by hand from the various objects they are attached to. Even the netspinners construct fine grained cases which are firmly attached to underwater objects before pupation, so at this time they must also be collected by hand.

If the angler can recognize the cases and the larvae of the important genera of caddisflies he will be able to discover which caddisflies are on his river and in what numbers. By dissecting the cases he will be able to discover which are in the pupation stage and how far along the process is. Armed with this knowledge he can then estimate when the next emergence will begin. Fortunately the cases of free-living larvae and net-spinning larvae are easy to identify to the genus level as they all have distinctive shapes. By comparing collected specimens to the pictures in this chapter the angler will be able to identify caddisfly larvae and cases from any trout stream in the country.

Drawings of Larvae and Cases of the Families

Fingernet Caddisflies. Family: Philopotamidae

FINGERNET LARVA

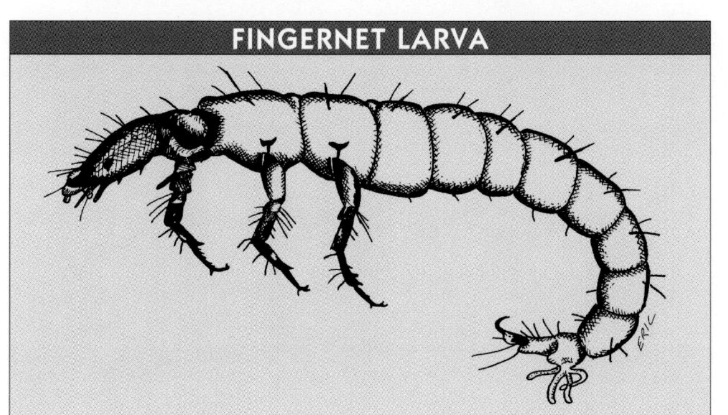

Trumpetnet and Tube-Making Caddisflies. Family: Polycentropodidae

TRUMPETNET LARVA

Nettube Caddisfly. Family: Psychomyiidae

NETTUBE LARVA

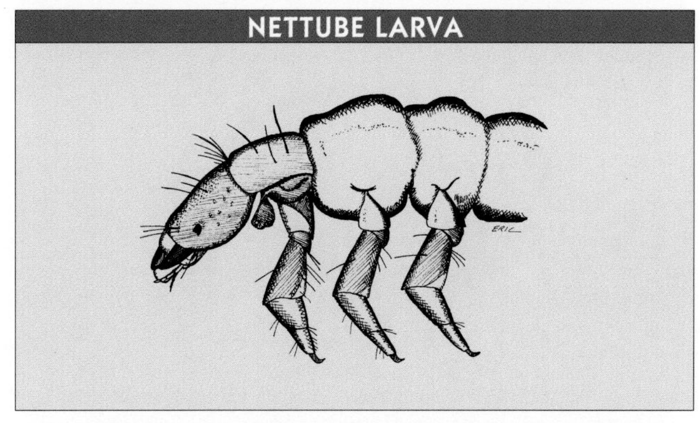

Common Netspinners. Family: Hydropsychidae

COMMON NETSPINNER LARVA

COMMON NETSPINNER CASE

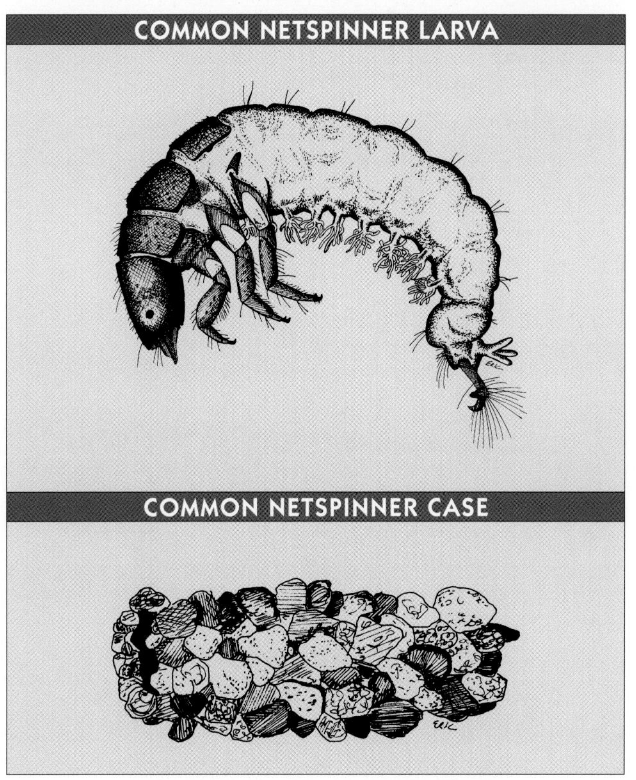

Saddle Case-Makers. Family: Glossosomatidae

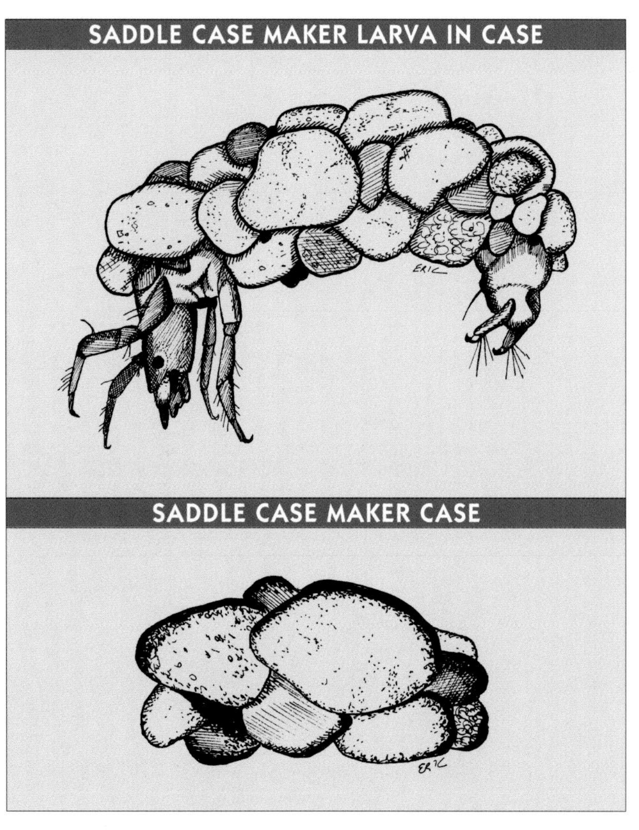

Humpless Case-Makers. Family: Brachycentridae

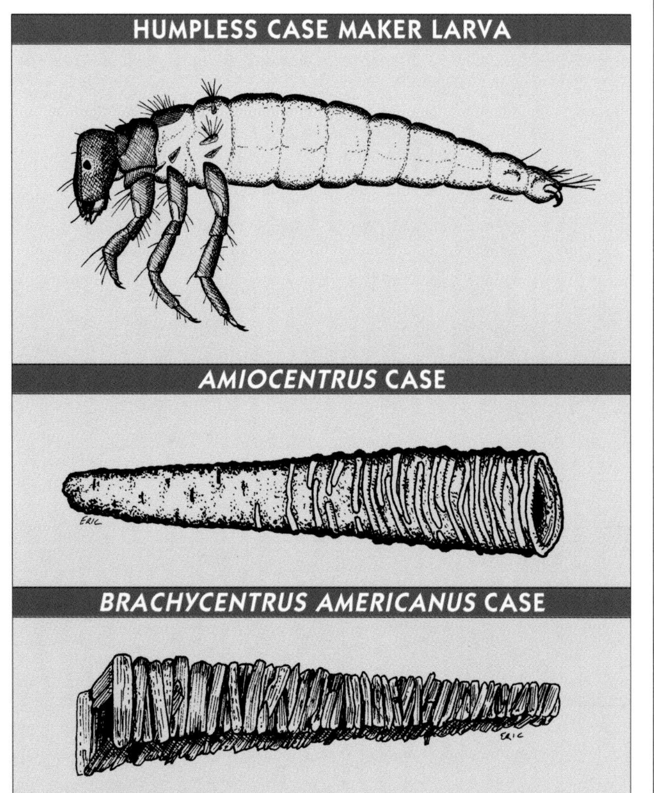

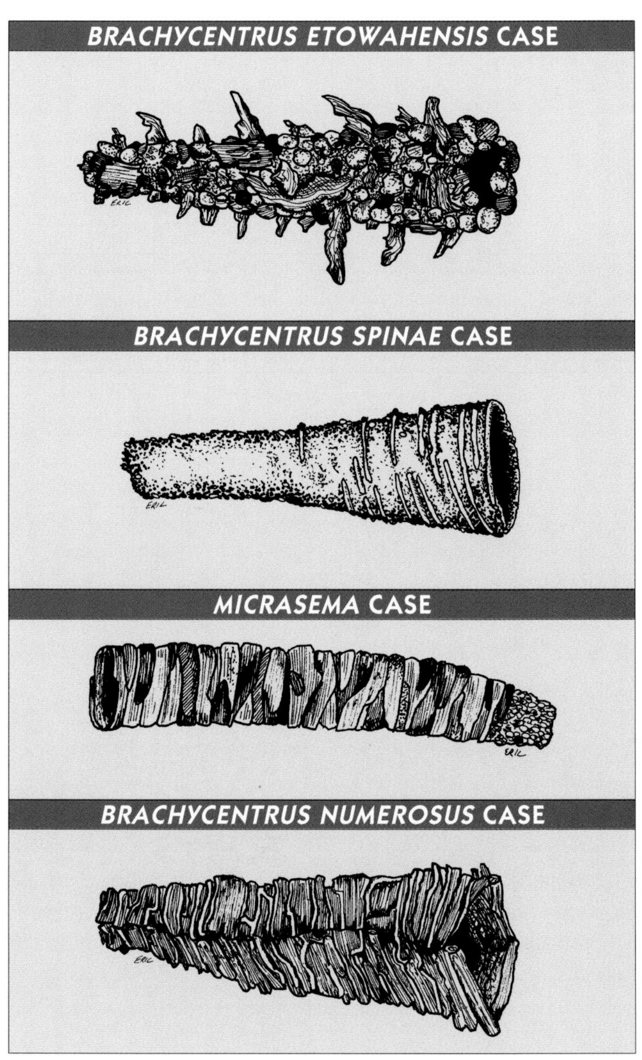

Strong Case-Makers. Family: Odontoceridae

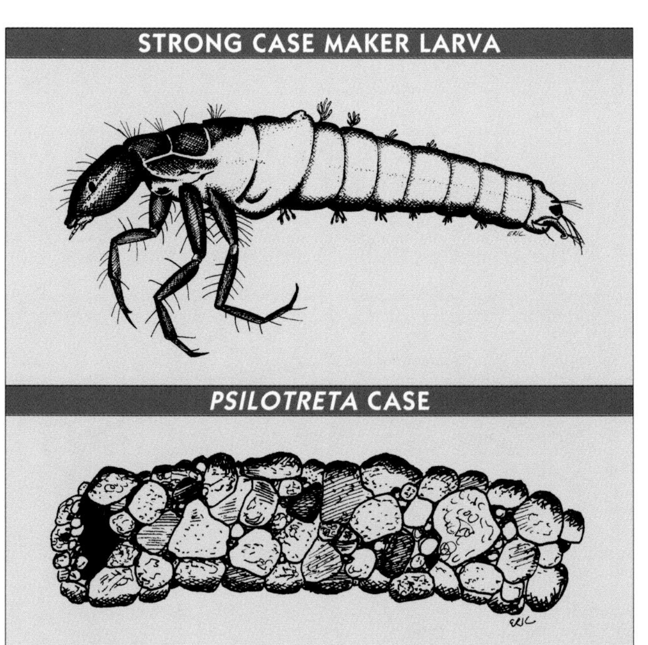

Lepidostomatid Case-Makers. Family: Lepidostomatidae

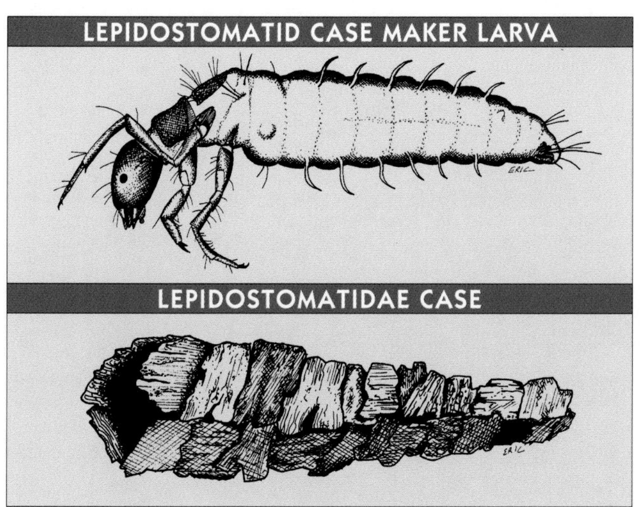

Long-Horned Case-Makers. Family: Leptoceridae

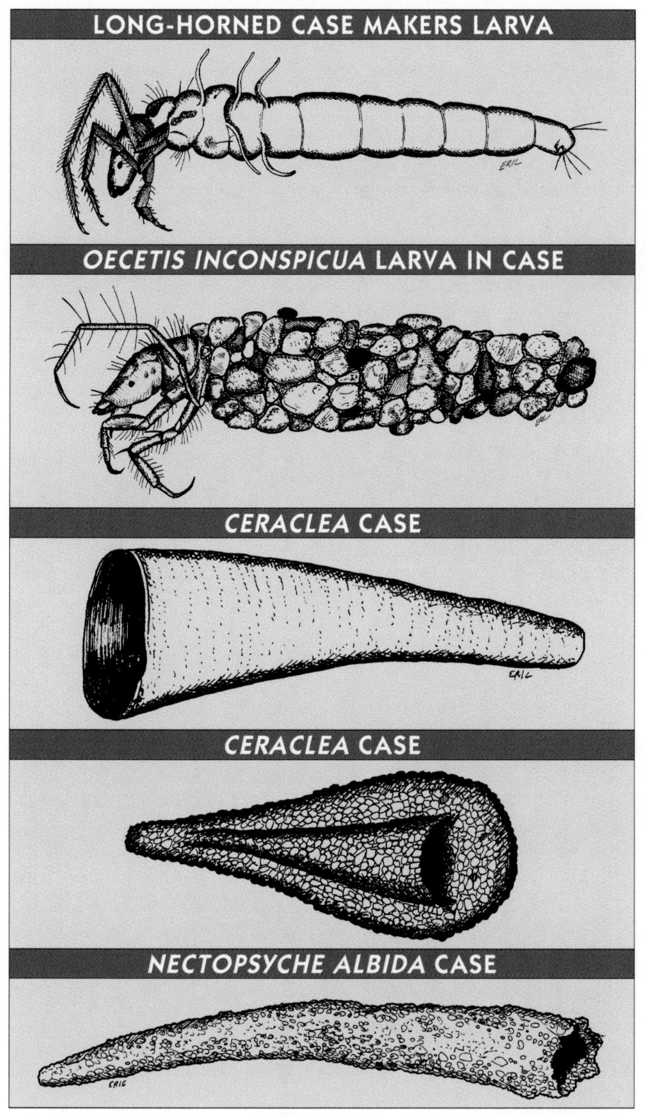

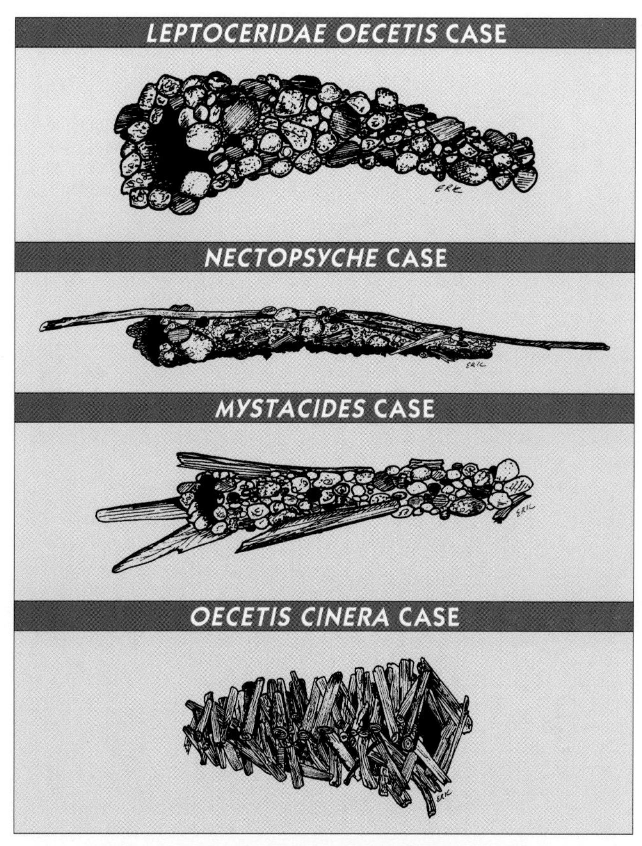

Hoodcase-Makers. Family: Molannidae

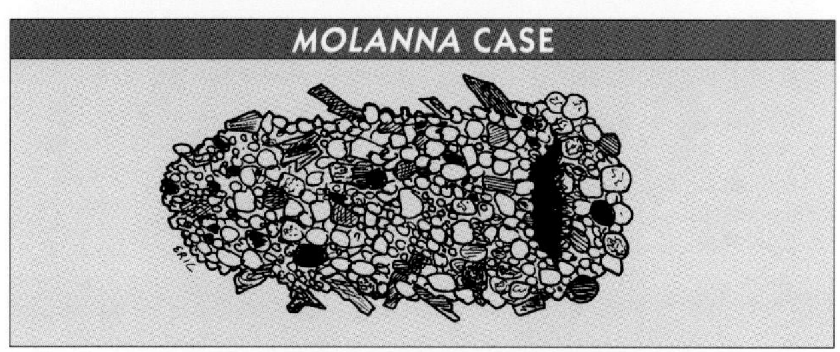

Microcaddisflies. Family: Hydroptilidae
Genera *Ochrotrichia, Oxyethira, Leucotrichia, Neotrichia*

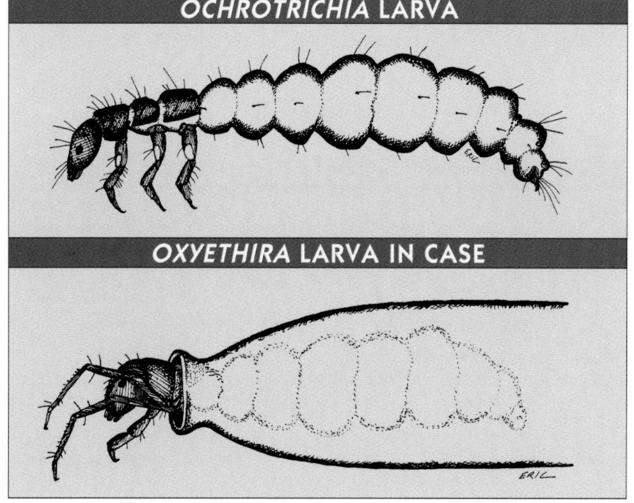

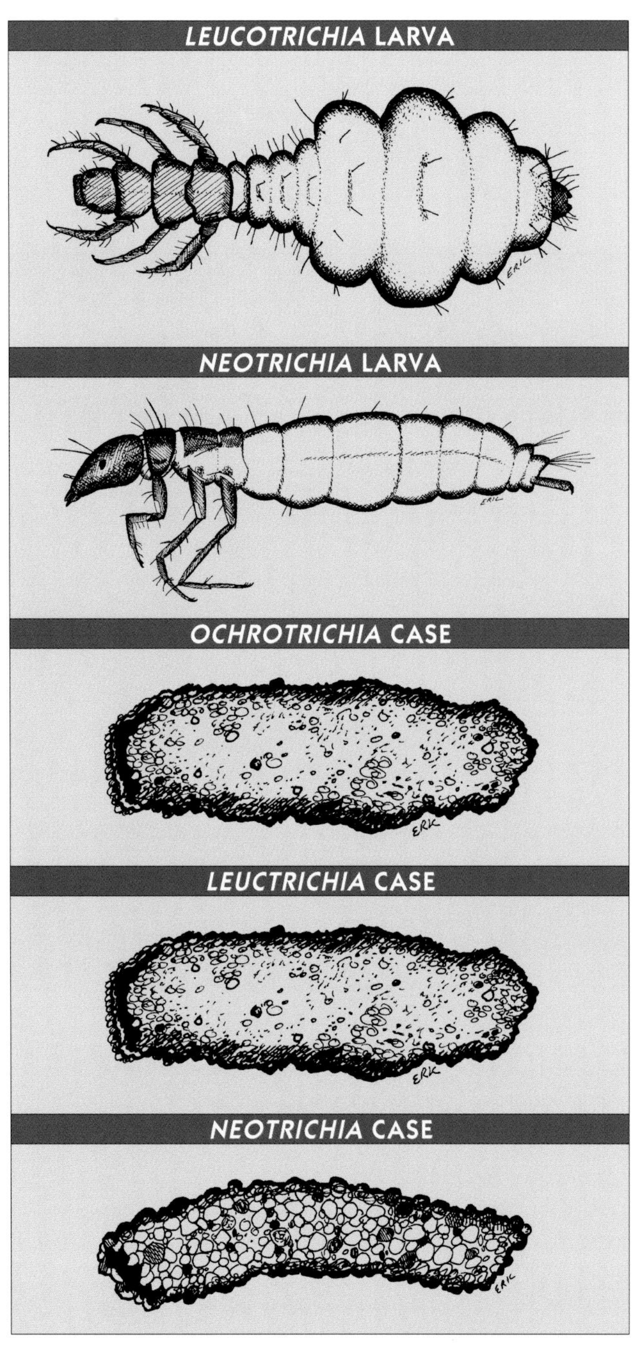

Giant Case-Makers. Family: Phryganeidae

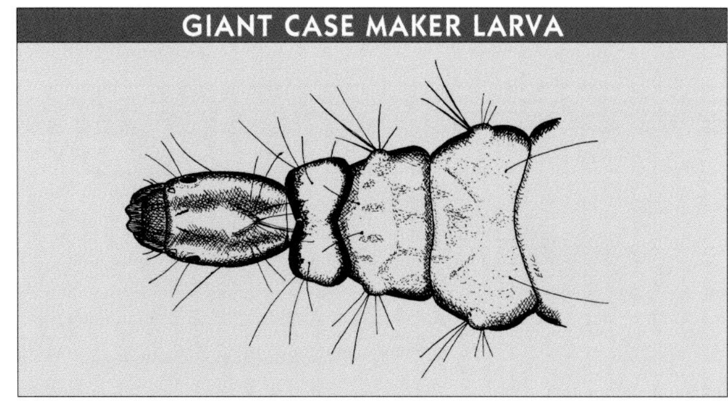

Northern Case-Makers. Family: Limnephilidae

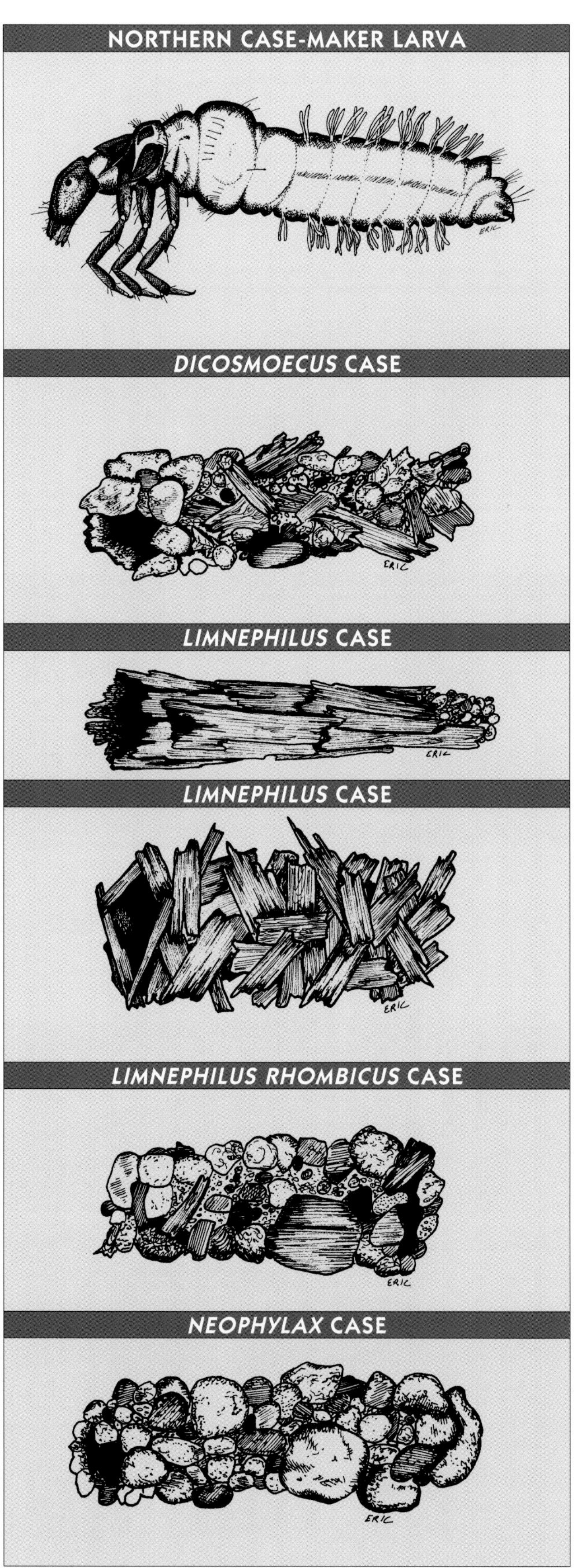

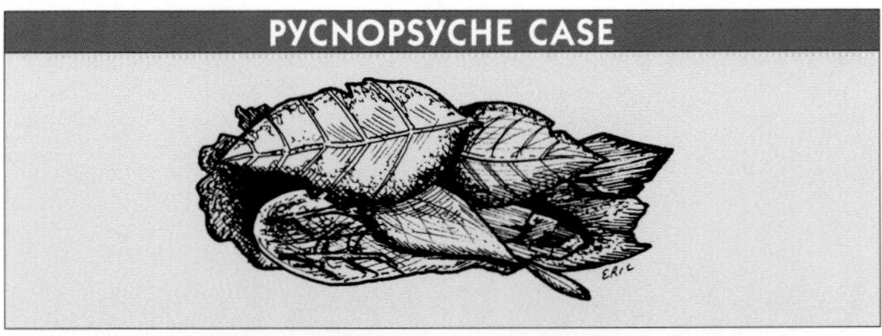

Free-Living Caddisflies. Family: Rhyacophilidae

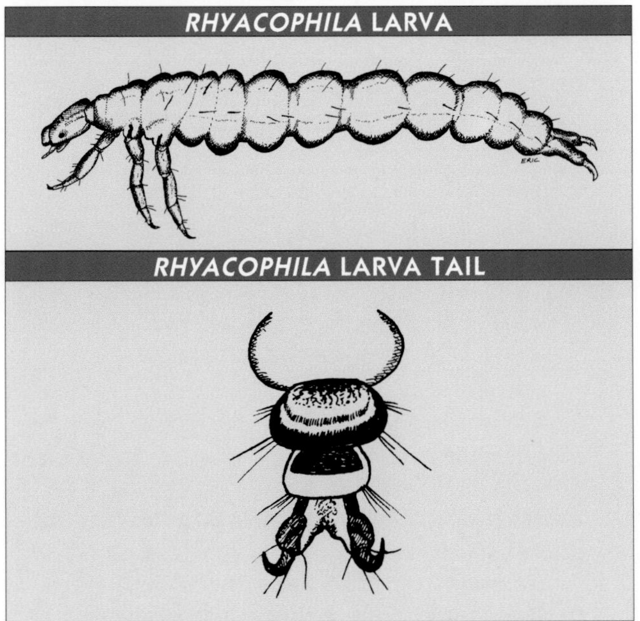

Snail Case-Makers. Family: Helicopsychidae

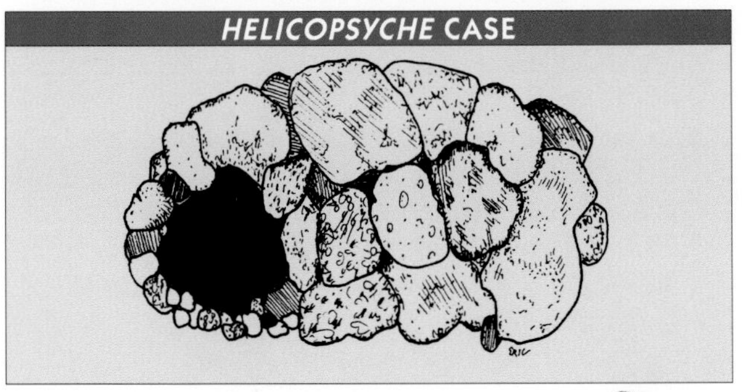

Chapter VII

KEYS TO IDENTIFYING TRAITS BY FAMILY AND GENERA

Keys to the Families of Trichoptera

1. Antennae more than twice as long as bodies. Bodies are slim, scutum has warts scattered in wide rows on either side (fig. 2). Long-Horned Case-Makers; Leptoceridae (Genera *Ceraclea, Nectopsyche, Mystacides, Oecetis*), Long-Horned Caddisflies medium sized, slim form with very long antennae.

   Antennae less than twice as long as body and very small, usually less than 5mm. 2

   Maxillary palps in five segments; segment five is twice the length of segment four (fig. 4). Usually longer than 5mm, wings not as narrow, without long fringes of hair. 3

   Segment five of maxillary palps not much longer than segment four and segments one and two are short and subequal in length (fig. 7). 4

   Female maxillary palps in five segments and male maxillary palps three or, rarely, two segments (fig. 9). 5

   Male maxillary palps in four segments, female maxillary palps in five segments (fig. 19). 6

   Anterior margin of hind wings has a row of modified hairs, 5mm to 7mm long (fig. 22). 7

   Scutellum is dome-like and a single wart occupies most of its area and its entire length (fig. 23), 12-14mm long. 8

   Antennae with scape at least three times longer than pedicel, 15-16mm long. 9

2. Less than 6mm long, usually less than 5mm long, very small and hairy, antennae shorter than forewings, wings are narrow and have long fringes of hair (fig. 3). Microcaddis; Hydroptilidae (Genera *Agraylea, Hydroptila, Leucotrichia, Oxyethira*). Microcaddisflies, tiny forms.

3. Maxillary palps in five segments; segment five is twice the length of segment four (fig. 4). Ocelli present (fig. 1), small dark forms. Fingernet Caddisflies; Philopotamidae (Genera *Chimarra, Dolophilodes, Wormaldia=Dolophilis*). Tiny Black Caddis, small, dark forms 6-8mm.

   Ocelli absent, maxillary palps in five segments; segment five is twice the length of segment four (fig. 4), segment five of maxillary palp is striated with a series of cross lines, scutum has warts (fig. 1), tibia of foreleg lacks a preapical spur (fig. 5). Nettube Caddisflies; Psychomyiidae (Genera *Lype, Psychomyia*). Dinky Purple-Breasted Sedge, body yellow, wings brown 5-6mm.

   Ocelli absent, maxillary palps in five segments; segment five is twice the length of segment four (fig. 4), scutum has warts (fig. 1), tibia of foreleg has a preapical spur, (fig. 5), those few without a preapical spur are distinguished from Nettube Caddisflies by the

relative lengths of segments two and three of maxillary palps, segment two is shorter than three. Trumpetnet and Tube-Making Caddisflies; Polycentropodidae (Genera *Neureclipsis, Nyctiophylax, Polycentropus*). Little Red Twilight Sedge, Dinky Light Summer sedge. Brown Checkered Summer Sedge, body yellowish, wings brown, plain or mottled, 5-9mm.

Maxillary palps in five segments; segment five is more than twice the length of segment four (fig. 4). Ocelli, warts of scutum and preapical spurs of forelegs all absent (fig. 6). Common Netspinners; Hydropsychidae (Genera, *Ceratopsyche, Hydropsyche, Cheumatopsyche, Macronema, Arctopsyche*). Cinnamon Sedge, Little Olive Sedge, Zebra Caddis, Great Gray Spotted Sedge, wide variation in size. 8-20mm.

4. Segment five of maxillary palp is not much longer than segment four, and segments one and two are short and subequal in length (fig. 7), ocelli present, tibia of forelegs has apical and preapical spurs (fig. 8). Free-Living Caddisflies; Rhyacophilidae (Genus *Rhyacophila*). Green Sedge, 8-13mm, occasionally larger.

Segment five of maxillary palps is not much longer than segment four, and segments one and two are short and subequal in length (fig. 7), tibia of foreleg lacks either apical or preapical spurs, or both. Saddle Case Maker; Glossosomatidae (Genera *Glossosoma* and *Protoptila*). Little Black Caddis, small, dark forms, 5-7.5mm.

Second genera *Pseudo* Microcaddis varied colors, 3-5.5mm.

5. Ocelli are absent, male maxillary palps in three or two segments, female palps in five segments, scutum has a pair of small, separated warts, scutellum has a larger pair of warts (fig. 10), tibia of middle leg has an irregular row of spines (fig. 11), preapical spurs on middle tibia 1/3 the way up from the apex of the tibia, or rarley without spurs; abdomen with opening of glands on center "V" in a pair of rounded, sclerotized lobes (fig. 12). Humpless Case-Makers; Brachycentridae (Genera *Brachycentrus, Amiocentrus, Micrasema*). Grannom, Little Black Caddis, 6-13mm.

Similar to Brachycentridae, male maxillary palps in three segments, female maxillary palps in five segments, male maxillary palps sometimes appear to be one segment, but the tibia of middle legs lack the row of spines and the preapical spurs of the tibia of the middle leg is 1/2 the way up from the apex of the tibia (fig. 13) Leptostomatid Case-Makers; Leptostomatidae (Genus *Lepidostoma*). Little Brown Sedge, wings brown sometimes with scales that look like spots and can be light or dark, body olive, 9-11mm.

Male maxillary palps in three segments, females five segments and second segment is much longer than first (fig. 14), mesoscutellum bearing a broad wart (fig. 15), tibia of foreleg has less than two spurs (fig. 16), or if more, then scutellum has a single oval wart, hind wings usually much wider than forewings (fig. 17), antennae with scape shorter than head (fig. 15). Northern Case-Makers; Limnephilidae (*Pycnopsyche, Chyranda, Hydratophylax, Frenesia, Platycentropus, Limnephilus, Hesperophylax, Pycnopsyche Dicosmoecus, Goera, Apatania, Neophylax* now uenoidae). Extremely variable forms from 5 to 30mm.

Same as above but hind wings are a little wider than fore-wings, antennae with scape longer than head (fig. 18), Uenoidae. Slender form, body length not exceeding 7mm. The exception are some species in Genera *Neophylax* which have recently been put in this family and do not follow the key very well. They key better to Limnephilidae (scape is like fig. 15), but they have a narrow mesoscutellar wart (fig. 18) instead of a broad scutellar wart (fig. 15). *Neophylax fuscous*, Small Dot Wing Sedge, 9-11mm.

6. Male maxillary palps in four segments, female palps in five segments, segment two much longer than segment one, and segment five not much longer than segment four (fig. 19). Tibia of forelegs has two or more spurs (fig. 20), ocelli present. Giant Case-Maker; Phryganeidae (Genera *Phryganea, Ptilostomis*). Large forms with patterned wings.

7. Scutellum has a single, narrow, transverse wart (fig. 21), anterior margin of hind wings has a row of modified hairs in the basal half and a slight concave in the distal half (fig. 22). Snail Case-Makers; Helicopsychidae (Genera *Helicopsyche*). Speckled Peter, tiny forms, body bright amber, wings light brown with heavy speckling of dark brown, 5-7mm.

8. Scutellum is dome-like and a single wart occupies most of its area and its entire length (fig. 23), maxillary palps always five segments. Strong Case-Makers; Odontoceridae (Genus *Psilotreta*). Dark Blue Sedge, 12-14mm.

9. Antennae with scape at least three times longer than pedicel, tibia of middle leg has a pair of preapical spurs and a row of 6-10 spines on the back side (fig. 24). Hood Case-Makers; Molannidae (Genus *Molanna*). Gray Checkered Sedge, 15-16mm.

FIGURE 1

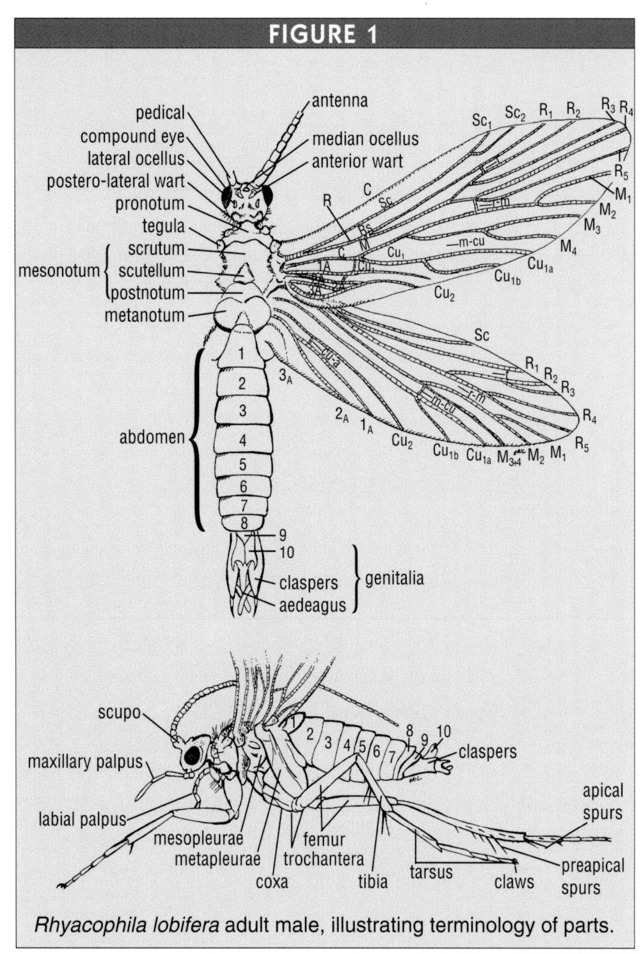

Rhyacophila lobifera adult male, illustrating terminology of parts.

FIGURE 2

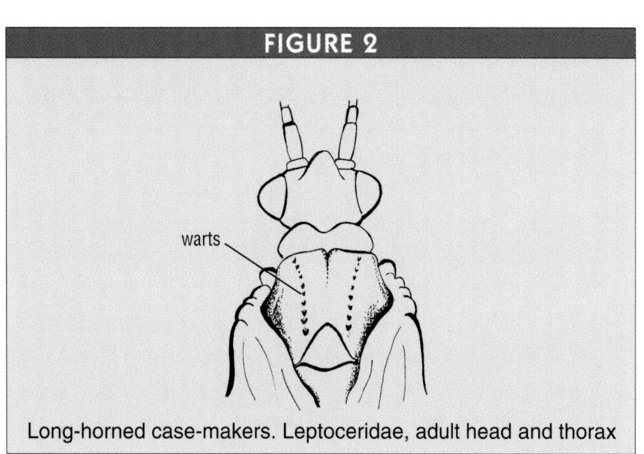

Long-horned case-makers. Leptoceridae, adult head and thorax

FIGURE 3

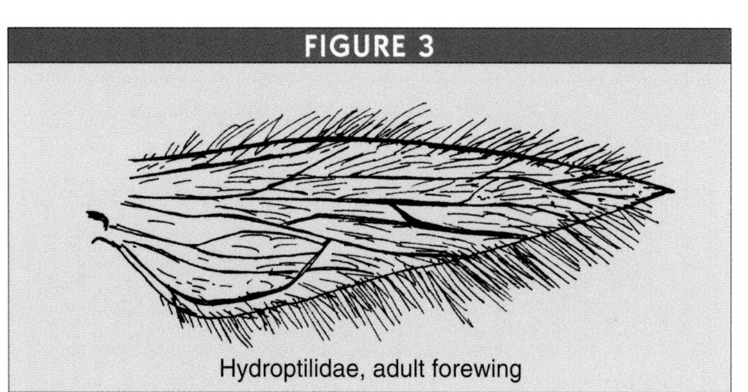

Hydroptilidae, adult forewing

FIGURE 4

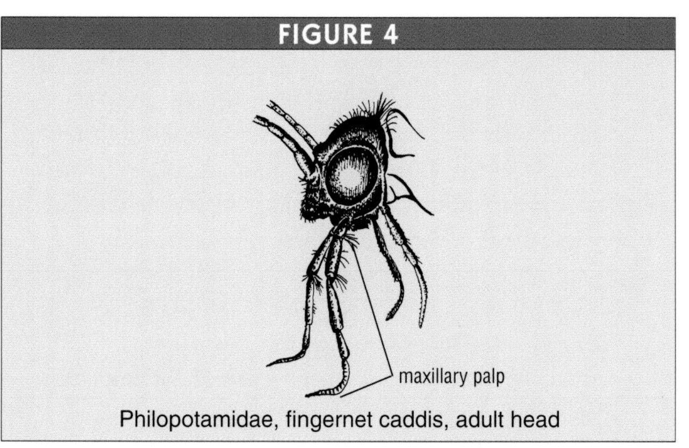

Philopotamidae, fingernet caddis, adult head

FIGURE 5

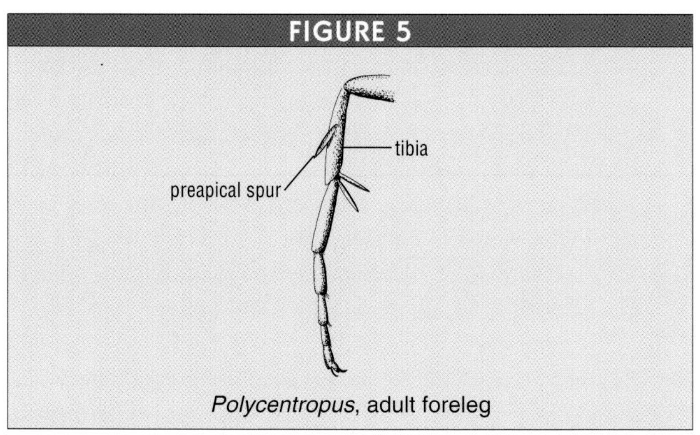

Polycentropus, adult foreleg

FIGURE 6

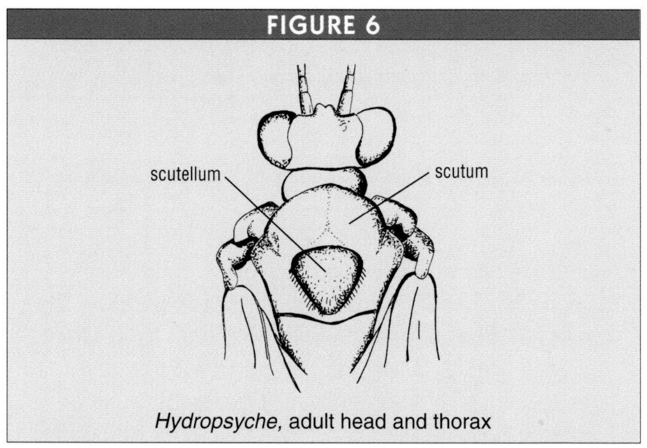

Hydropsyche, adult head and thorax

FIGURE 7

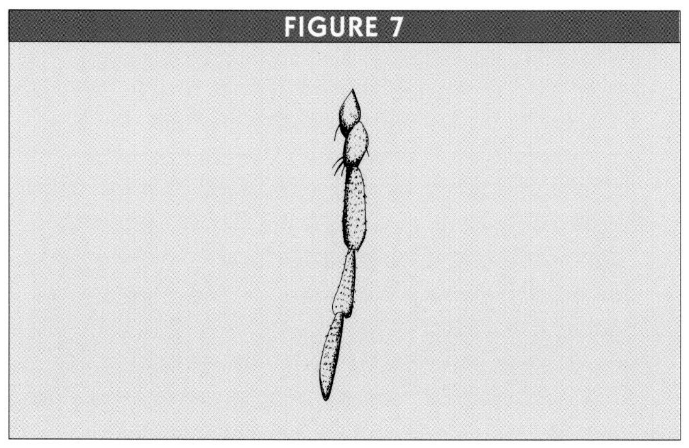

FIGURE 8

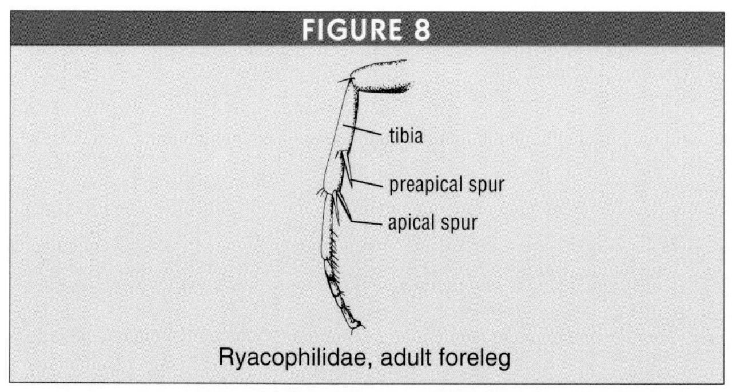
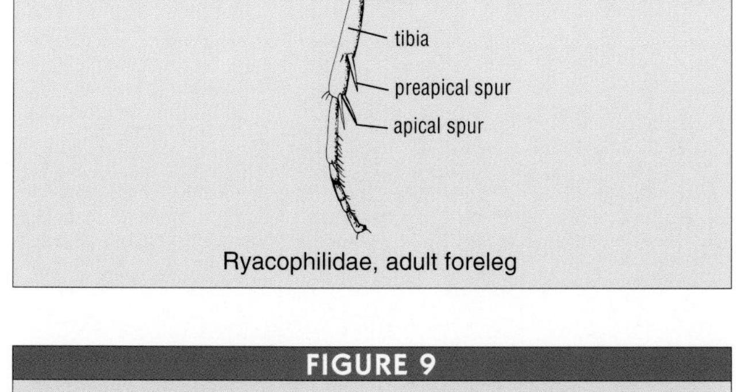

Ryacophilidae, adult foreleg

FIGURE 9

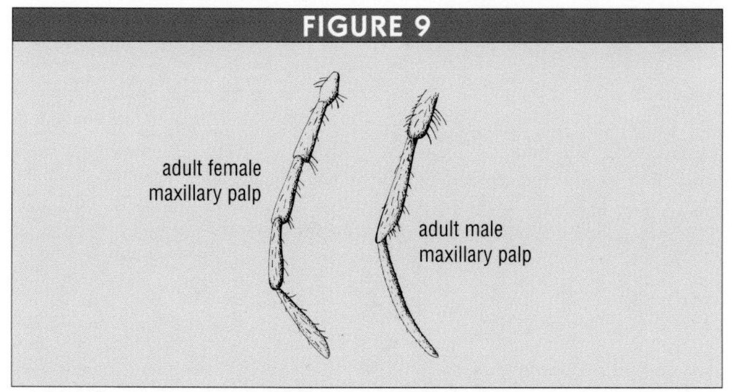

FIGURE 10

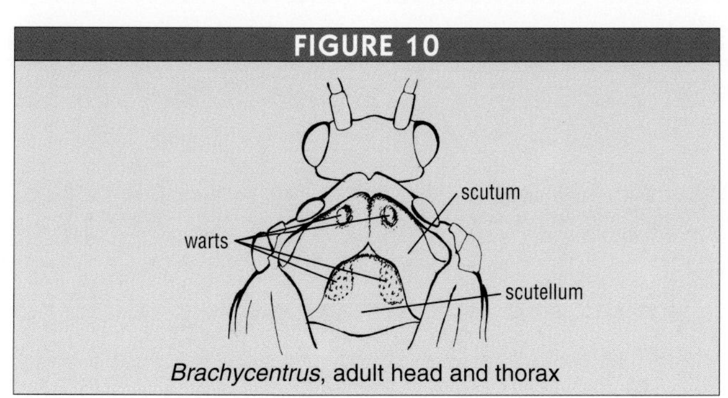

Brachycentrus, adult head and thorax

FIGURE 11

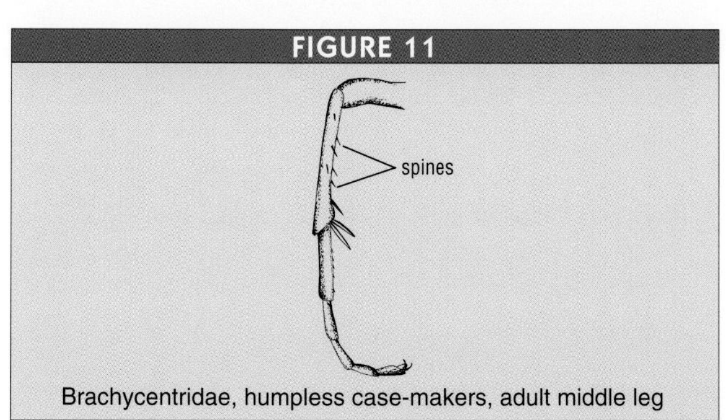

Brachycentridae, humpless case-makers, adult middle leg

FIGURE 12

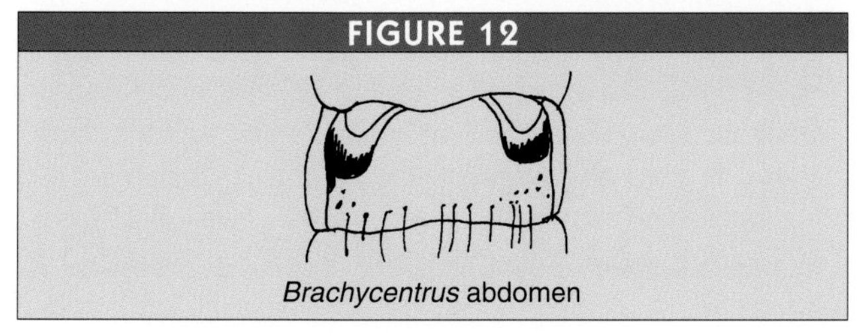

Brachycentrus abdomen

FIGURE 13

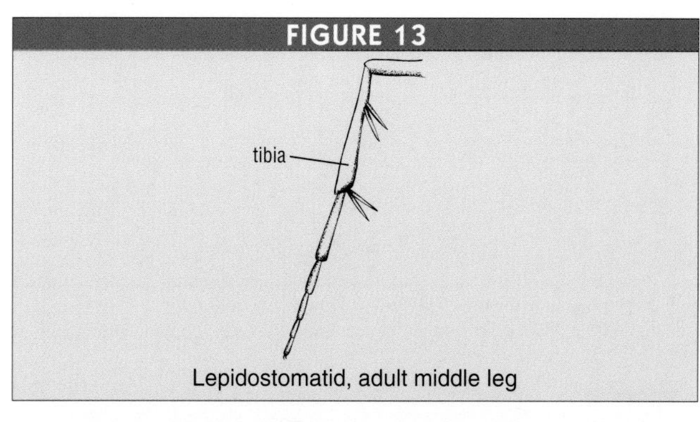

Lepidostomatid, adult middle leg

FIGURE 14

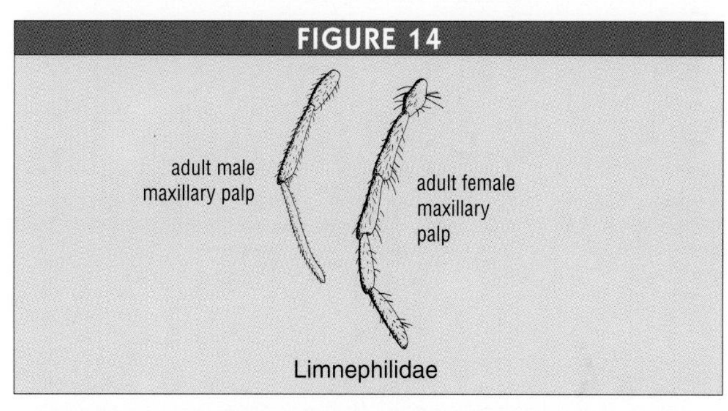

Limnephilidae

FIGURE 15

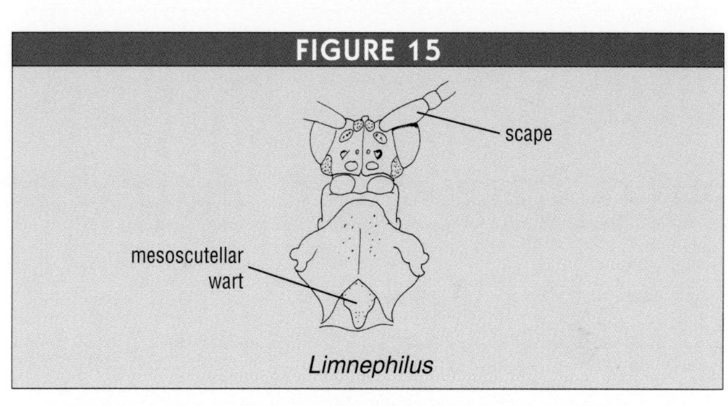

Limnephilus

FIGURE 16

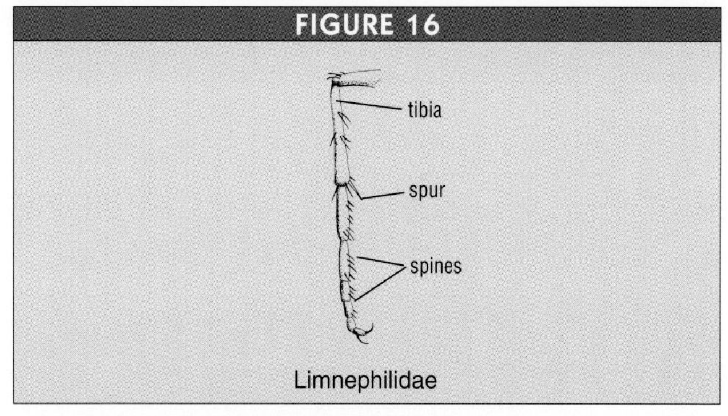

Limnephilidae

FIGURE 17

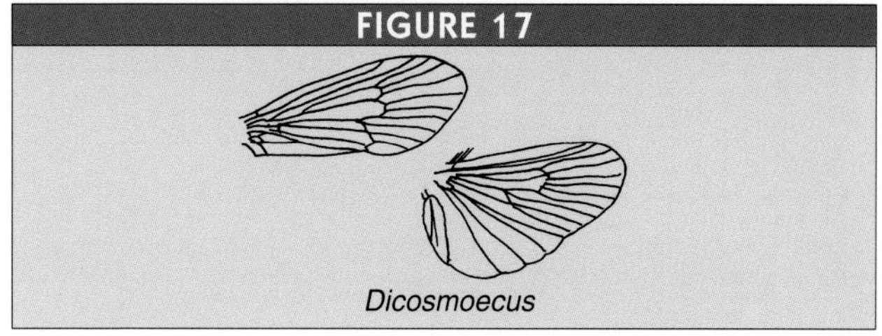

Dicosmoecus

FIGURE 18

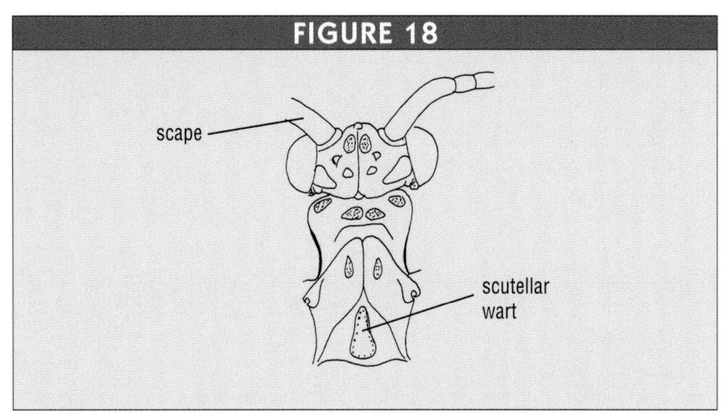

FIGURE 19

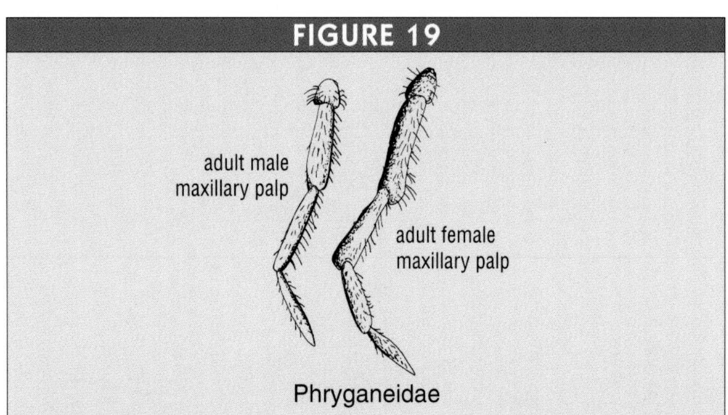

Phryganeidae

FIGURE 20

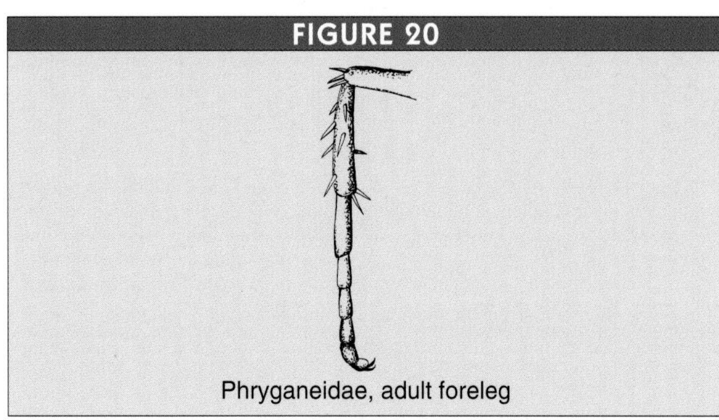

Phryganeidae, adult foreleg

FIGURE 21

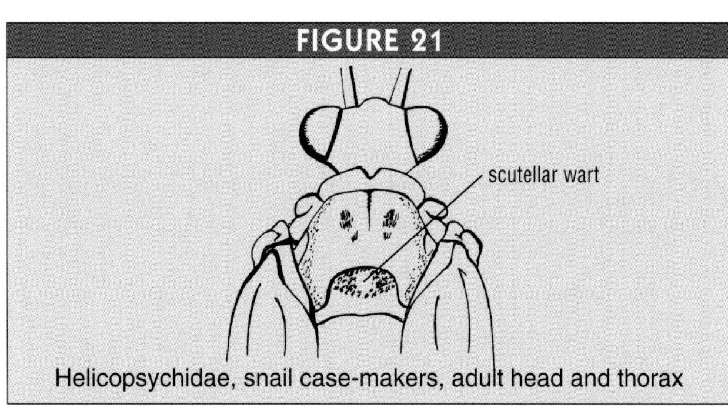

Helicopsychidae, snail case-makers, adult head and thorax

FIGURE 22

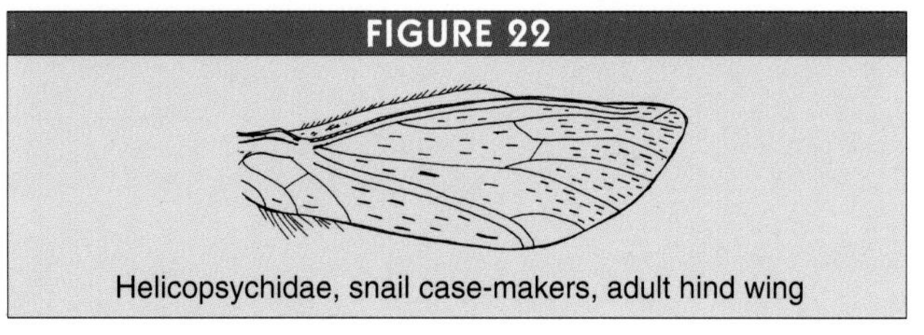

Helicopsychidae, snail case-makers, adult hind wing

FIGURE 23

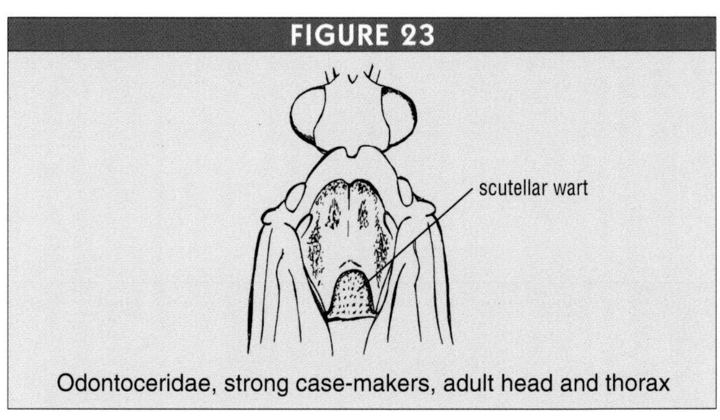

Odontoceridae, strong case-makers, adult head and thorax

FIGURE 24

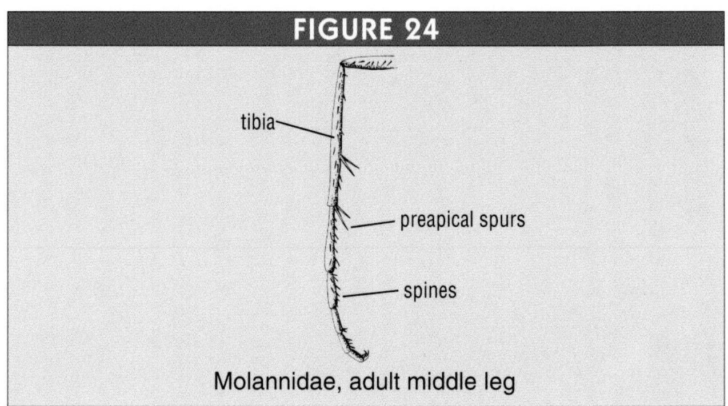

Molannidae, adult middle leg

Keys to the Genera of Brachycentridae (Adults)

1. Spurs 2, 4, 4; *Eobrachycentrus*
   Spurs 2, 2, 2 or 2, 2, 3 or 2, 3, 3 2

2. R1 of forewing with a kink at level of cord, fig. 1 3
   R1 of forewing straight or slightly sinuate to margin, fig. 2 4

3. Maxillary palps of male in two segments; spurs 2, 2, 2—*Amiocentrus.* Maxillary palps of male in three-segmented; spurs generally 2, 2, 2, rarely 2, 2, 3 or 2, 2, 2—*Brachycentrus*

4. Forewing with R4+5 forked at S—*Adicrophleps*
   Forewing with R4+5 forked distinctly beyond S, fig. 2—*Micrasema*

   (Spurs 2, 2, 3 means the first leg has two apical spurs on the tibia, the second leg has the same, and the third leg has two apical spurs and a preapical spur on the tibia and so on, no tibia has more than two apical spurs, so any number higher than two refers to preapical spurs).

FIGURE 1

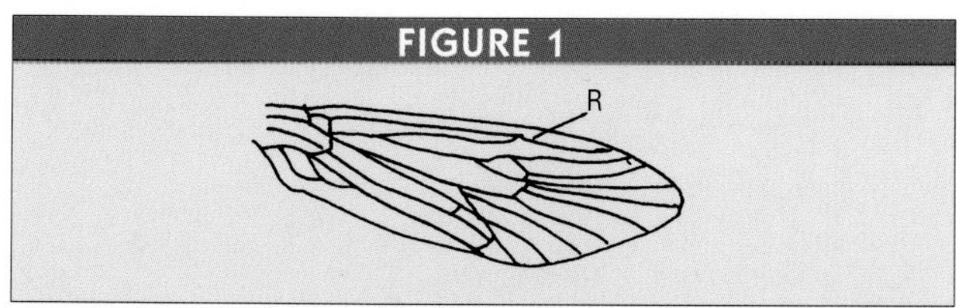

FIGURE 2

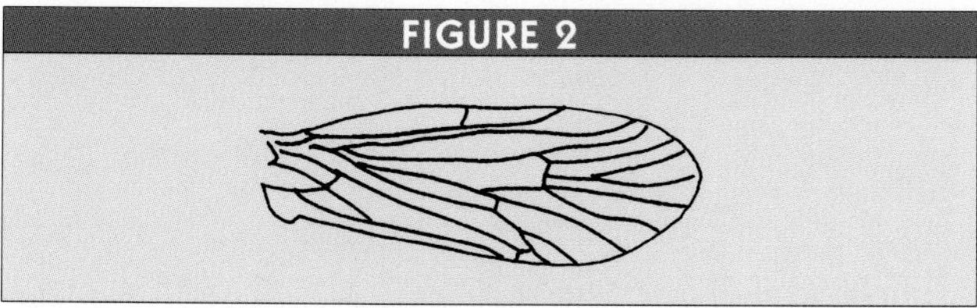

Keys to the Genera of Philopotamidae (Adults)

1. Wings reduced to stubs, fig.1; *Dolophilodes.*
   Wings normal 2

2. Front tibia with one apical spur; *Chimarra.*
   Front tibia with two apical spurs 3

3. Front wings with vein R2+3 branching beyond radial cross-veins, near margin of wing, fig. 2; *Dolophilodes.*
   Front wings with vein R2+3 branching at or near radial cross-veins or not branched; *Dolophilus=Wormaldia.*

FIGURE 1

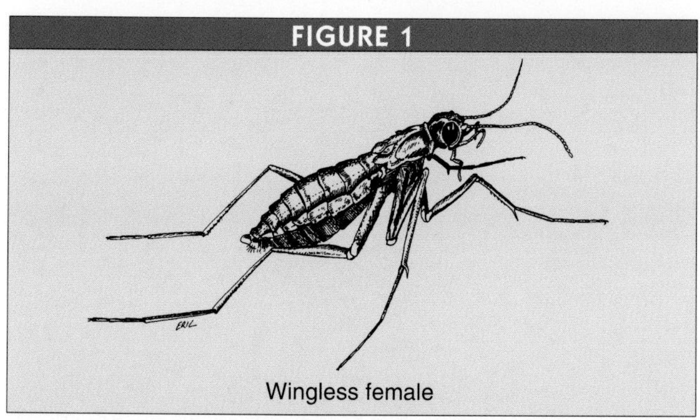

Wingless female

FIGURE 2

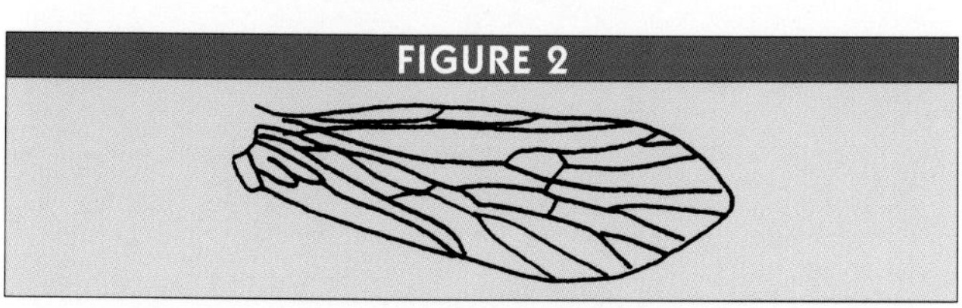

FIGURE 3

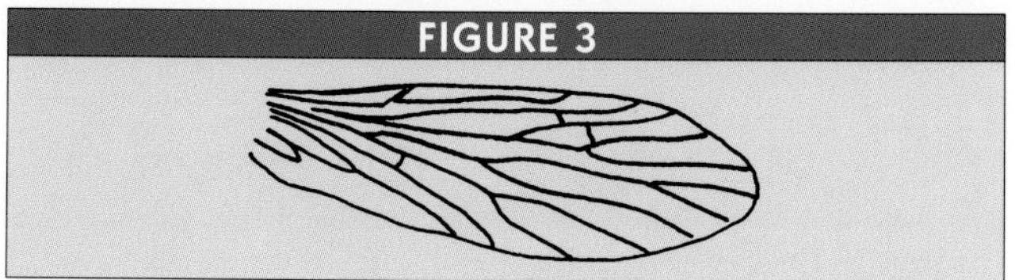

Keys to the Genera of Hydropsychidae (Adults)

1. Head with anterior warts large and swollen, posterior warts much smaller, fig.1; this is a large species from large rapid rivers in the Midwest and East, with very long antennae and pictured wings. 15-18mm, wings dark brown showing a pattern of yellow, as in fig. 2; *Macronema.*

FIGURE 1

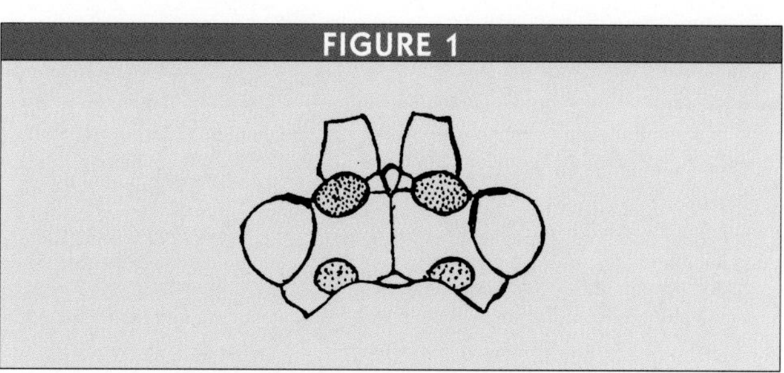

FIGURE 2

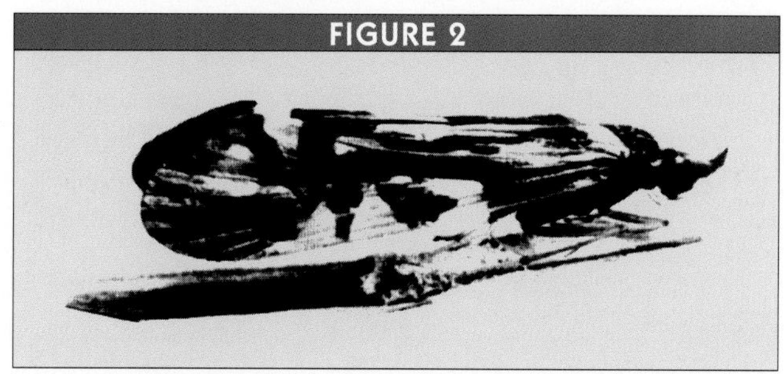

2. Middle tibia greatly widened and flattened, fig. 3, second segment of maxillary palpi distinctly shorter than third segment, fig. 4.
   This is a large western species (up to 20mm), from brownish-olive to bright olive bodies depending on the river, with brown wings spotted with darker brown; *Arctopsyche.*

FIGURE 3

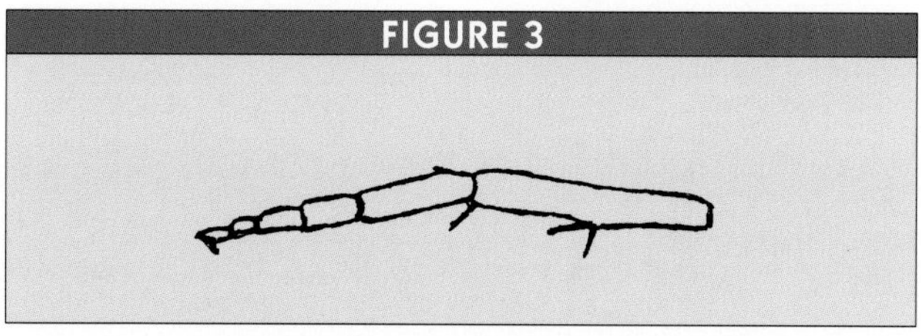

FIGURE 4

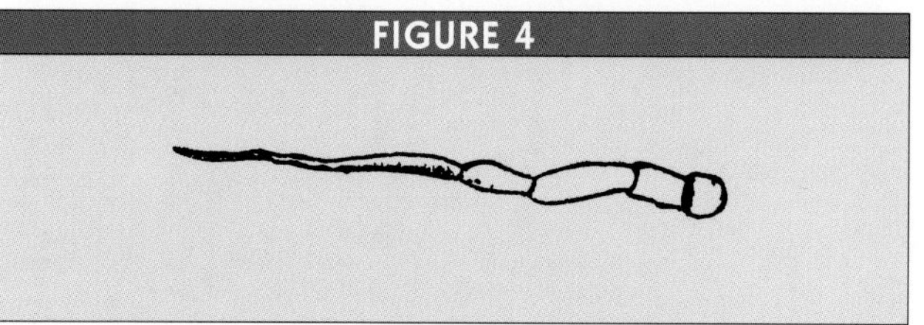

3. Males front tibia without apical spurs, fig. 5; body and wings straw colored with tawny or light brown on dorsum, 10-11mm. Common large stream insect in the Midwest; *Potamyia flava.*

FIGURE 5

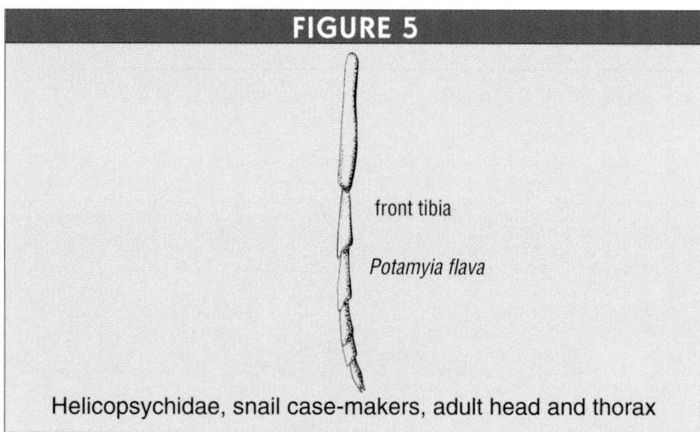

Helicopsychidae, snail case-makers, adult head and thorax

4. Male: Base of aedeagus cylindrical, figs. 6-7, Females: sternal plates of eighth segment separated only two-thirds the distance to base of segment, fig. 8; *Ceratopsyche* and *Hydropsyche*. *Ceratopsyche* used to be in *Hydropsyche*. Many insects in the present *Hydropsyche* have tan markings in the middle of the top of the wing. *Ceratopsyche* have grayish-brown wings with little tan spots which are scattered over the entire wing.

FIGURE 6

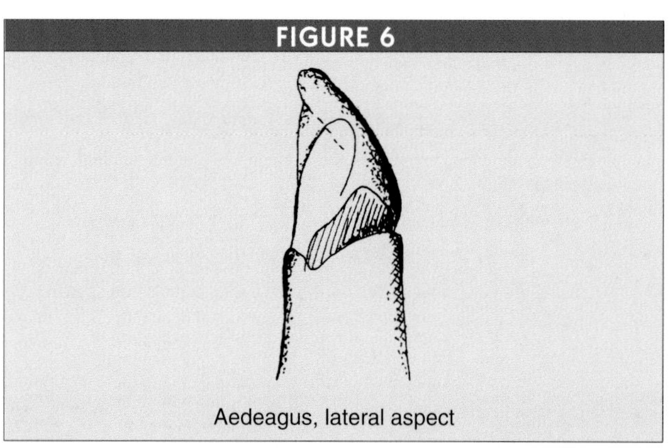

Aedeagus, lateral aspect

FIGURE 7

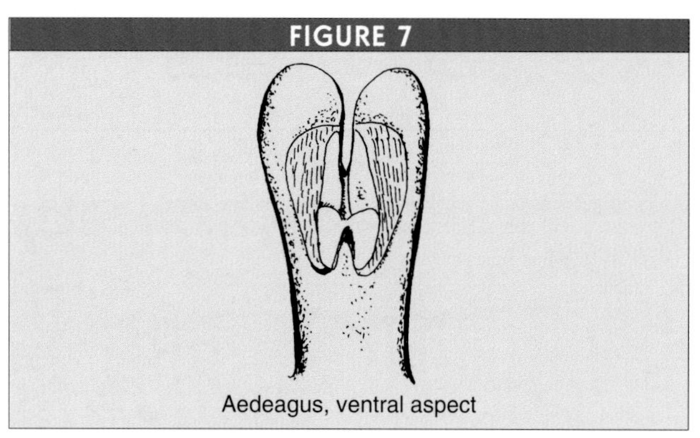

Aedeagus, ventral aspect

FIGURE 8

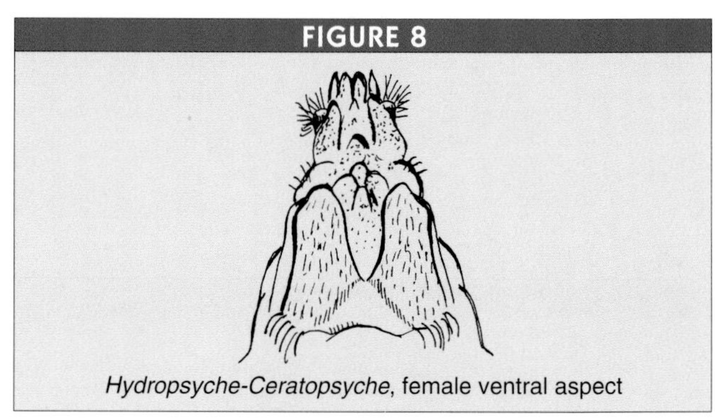

Hydropsyche-Ceratopsyche, female ventral aspect

5. Male: Base of aedeagus bulbous, fig. 9; Female: sternal plates of eighth segment separated to base of segment, fig. 10. *Cheumatopsyche.*

FIGURE 9

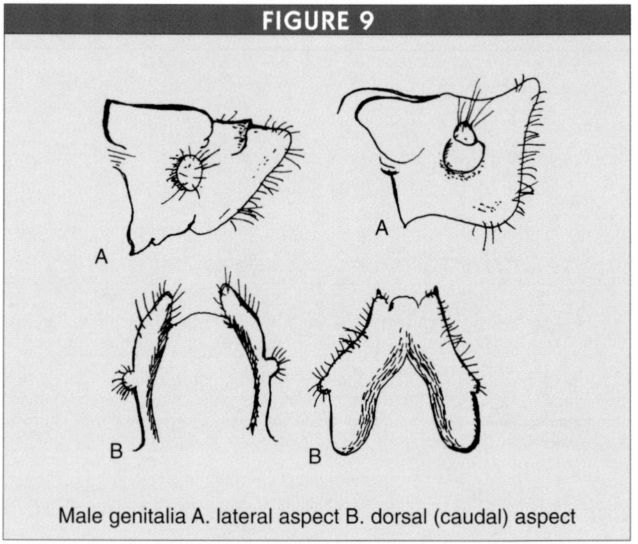

Male genitalia A. lateral aspect B. dorsal (caudal) aspect

FIGURE 10

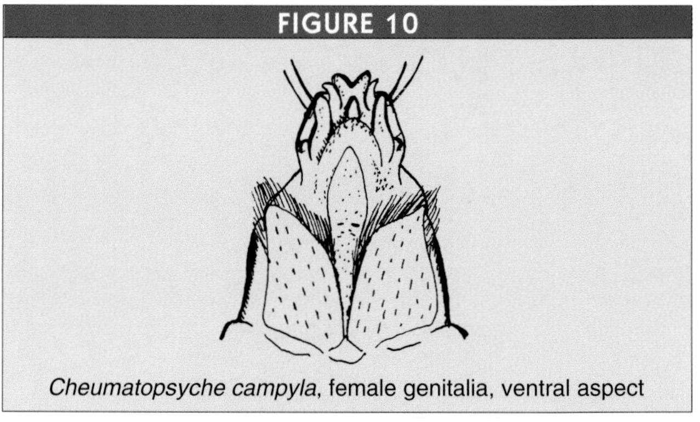

Cheumatopsyche campyla, female genitalia, ventral aspect

Key to the Genera of Leptoceridae (Adults)

1. Front wings with stem of M atrophied, leaving only two main veins between convex R 1 and convex Cu 1, fig. 1. *Triaenodes.*

(These are usually not found in trout streams, they usually have black and cream patterns in the wings.)
Front wings with stem of M present, so that three main veins are present between convex R1 and convex Cu1, fig. 2. 2

FIGURE 1

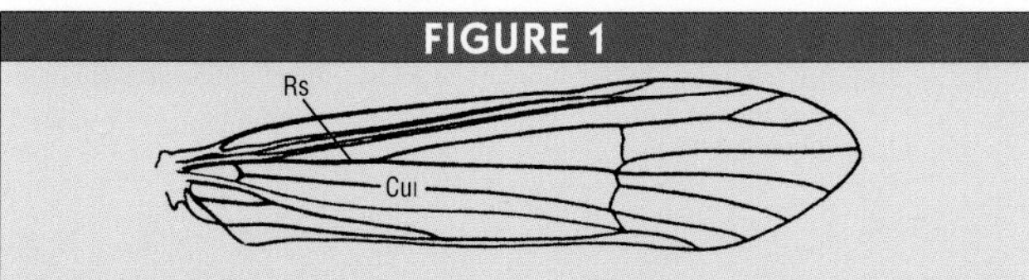

FIGURE 2

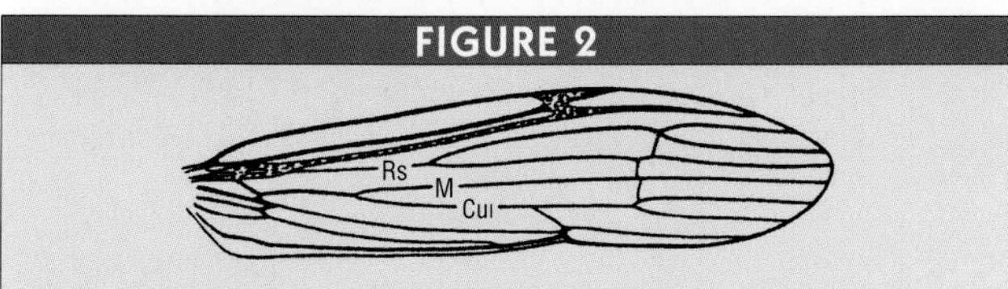

2. M apparently not branched, fig. 2.; *Oecetis.*
(These are usually medium red-brown to tan with plain wings or with a few small black spots.)
M obviously branched, fig. 3. 3

FIGURE 3

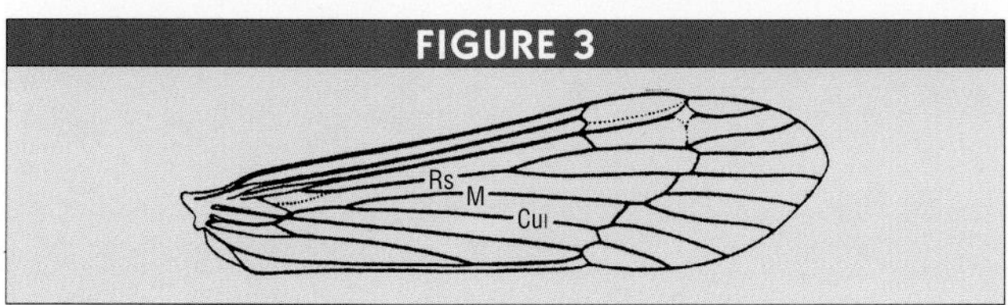

3. Epicranial stem distinct, lateral sutures absent or indistinct, fig. 4. 4

FIGURE 4

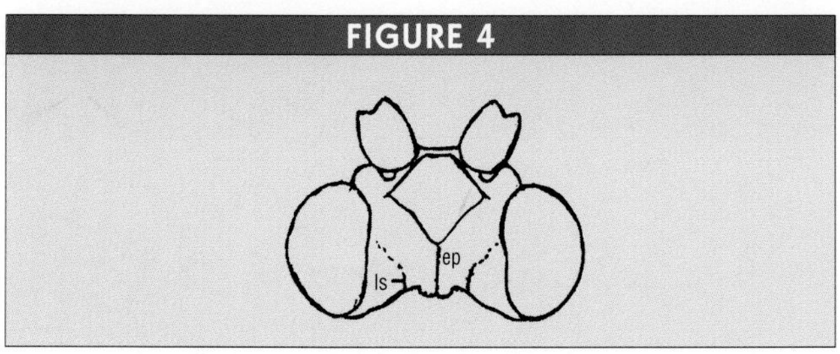

Epicranial stem absent or indistinct, lateral sutures well marked, fig. 5. 5

FIGURE 5

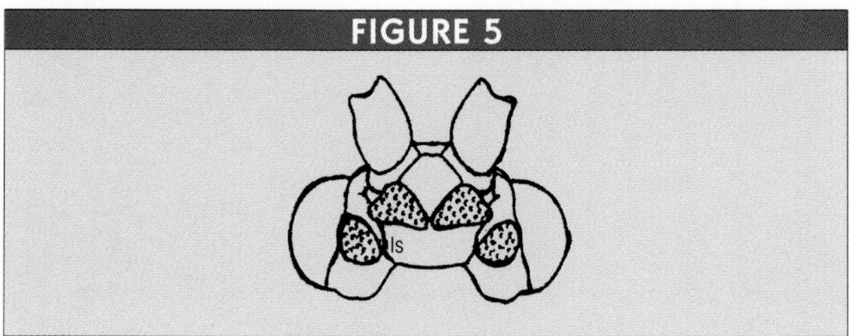

4. Dorsal triangle of head small, epicranial stem long, fig. 6, color whitish, straw yellow or light brown; *Setodes.*
(Usually not found on trout streams.)

FIGURE 6

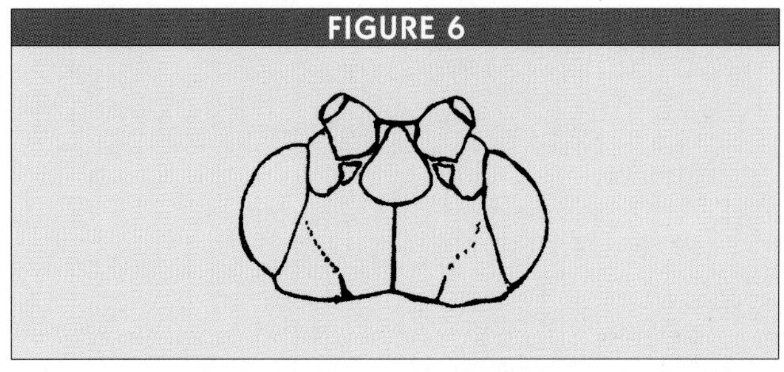

Dorsal triangle of head large, epicranial stem short, fig. 4, color very dark brown or bluish-black including wings; *Mystacides.*

FIGURE 4

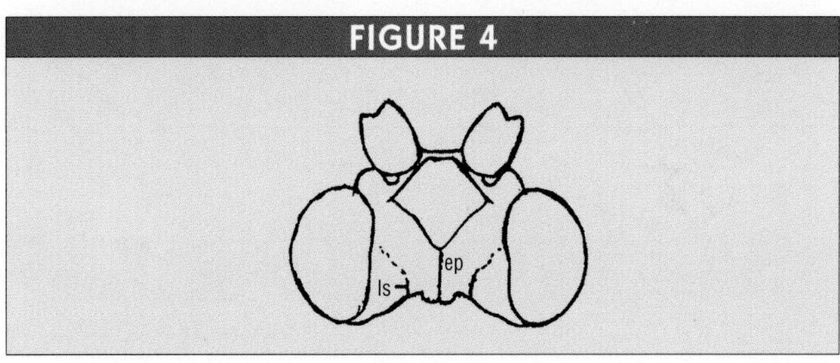

5. Hind wings with most of Rs and its branches atrophied, ground color white; *Leptocella.*
Hind wings with Rs and its branches present, ground color not white. 6

6. Front tibia with two apical spurs; *Ceraclea.*
(These are usually brown to black often with cream or tan scales and dark gray or green bodies)
Front tibia without apical spurs; *Leptocerus.*
(These are a lake species found in trout lakes.)

Bibliography

Flint, O. S. Jr, 1984, "The Genus *Brachycentrus* in North America, with a Proposed Phylogeny of the Genera of Brachycentridae (Trichoptera)" Smithsonian Institution Press, City of Washington, Smithsonian Contributions to Zoology, Number 398

Juracek, John, and Craig Mathews, 1992, *Fishing the Yellowstone Hatches.* Blue Ribbon Flies, West Yellowstone, Montana.

LaFontaine, Gary, 1981, *Caddisflies.* Nick Lyons/Winchester Press, New York, N.Y.

Leonard, J. W. and F.A. Leonard, 1949, "An Annotated List of Michigan Trichoptera." Occasional Papers of the Museum of Zoology, 522.

—1949, "Noteworthy Records of Caddis Flies from Michigan, with Descriptions of New Species." Papers of the Museum of Zoology, University of Michigan.

McCafferty, W. Patrick, 1981, *Aquatic Entomology.* Jones and Bartlett Publishers, Inc., Boston, MA.

Ross H. H., 1944, "The Caddisflies or Trichoptera of Illinois." State of Illinois Natural History Survey Division, Volume 23.

Ross, H. H. and J.D. Unzicker, 1965, "The *Micrasema Rusticum* Group of Caddisflies (Brachycentridae, Trichoptera)." Proceedings of the Biological Society of Washington. 78:251-258.

Shewey, John, 1994, *Mastering The Spring Creeks.* Frank Amato Publications, Inc., Portland, OR.

Solomon, Larry and Eric Leiser, 1977, *The Caddis and the Angler.* Stackpole Books, Harrisburg, PA.

Wiggins, G. B., 1977, *Larvae of the North American Caddisfly Genera (Trichoptera).* Toronto and Buffalo: University of Toronto Press.

—1978, "Trichoptera." In R.W. Merritt and K.W. Cummins, Editors, *An Introduction to the Aquatic Insects of North America*, pages 147-185. Kendall/Hunt Publishing Company. Dubuque, IA.

Index

Italics indicate genera

STREAMSIDE NOTES FOR CADDISFLY IDENTIFICATION

Wings	Length	Color	Shape (which type)
Body	Length	Color	Shape (slim or robust)
Legs	Color		
Antennae	Length (in relation to body and wing)		Color

HOOK SIZE TO OVERALL LENGTH FOR CADDISFLY IMITATION

Overall Length = Body Length = Hook Size

Overall Length	Body Length	Hook Size
❏ 6mm	4mm	22
❏ 8mm	5mm	20
❏ 10mm	6mm	18
❏ 13mm	7mm	16
❏ 16mm	9.5mm	14
❏ 20mm	11mm	12
❏ 24mm	13mm	10
❏ 29mm	15mm	8

MILLIMETERS
0 5 10 15 20 25 30 35 40 45 50 55

These numbers are approximate depending on species of caddisfly and type of hook. It is best to measure hook length and if possible length of the natural's body and total length.

COLOR CHARTS FOR CADDISFLY BODIES

❏ Cinnamon brown for Cinnamon Sedge and other patterns listed as cinnamon.

❏ Green for Green Sedge and Little Green Sedge

❏ Green for White Miller

❏ Ginger for White Miller thorax

❏ Gray for Little Black Caddis and other patterns listed as dark gray.

❏ Tan for patterns listed as tan.

Caddisfly bodies can vary in color depending on river, time elapsed after emergence, and age of underlying egg mass and sperm. These colors are a recommended starting point only.

LEARN MORE ABOUT FLY FISHING AND FLY TYING WITH THESE BOOKS

If you are unable to find the books shown below at your local book store or fly shop you can order direct from the publisher below.

Flies: The Best One Thousand
Randy Stetzer
$24.95

Fly Tying Made Clear and Simple
Skip Morris
$19.95 (HB: $29.95)

The Art of Tying the Dry Fly
Skip Morris
$29.95(HB:$39.95)

Curtis Creek Manifesto
Sheridan Anderson
$7.95

American Fly Tying Manual
Dave Hughes
$9.95

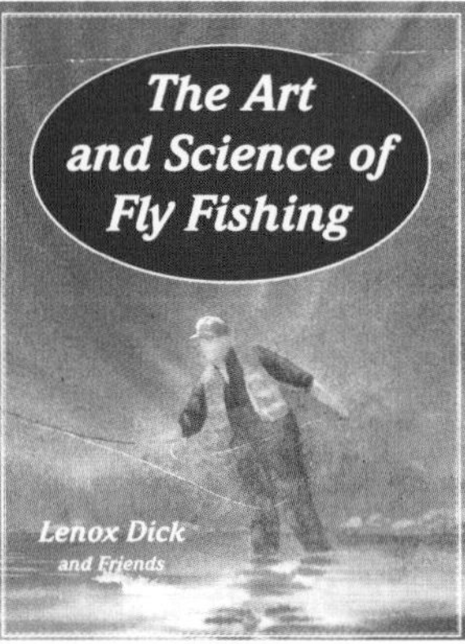

The Art and Science of Fly Fishing
Lenox Dick
$19.95

Western Hatches
Dave Hughes, Rick Hafele
$24.95

Lake Fishing with a Fly
Ron Cordes, Randall Kaufmann
$26.95

Advanced Fly Fishing for Steelhead
Deke Meyer
$24.95

Fly Patterns of Alaska
Alaska Flyfishers
$19.95

Fly Tying & Fishing for Panfish and Bass
Tom Keith
$19.95

Float Tube Fly Fishing
Deke Meyer
$11.95

VISA, MASTERCARD or AMERICAN EXPRESS ORDERS CALL TOLL FREE: 1-800-541-9498
(9-5 Pacific Standard Time)

Or Send Check or money order to:

Frank Amato Publications
Box 82112
Portland, Oregon 97282

(Please add $3.00 for shipping and handling)